HOPI

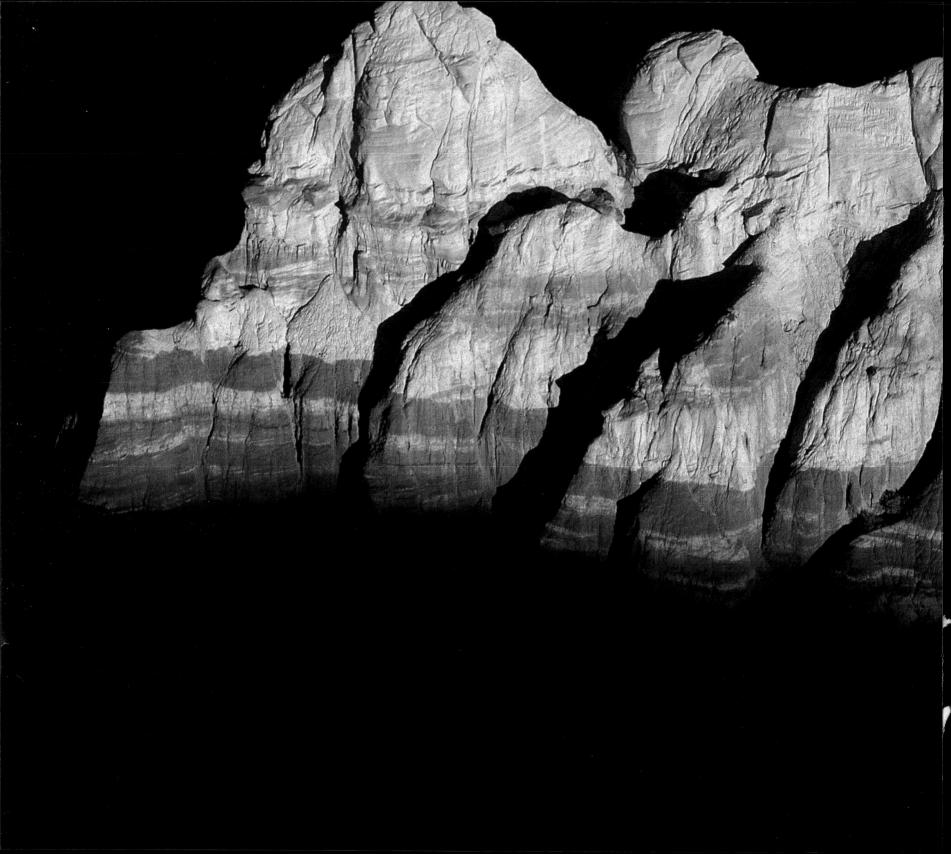

HOPI

SUSANNE AND JAKE PAGE

·

RIO NUEVO PUBLISHERS

TUCSON, ARIZONA

CONTENTS

PREFACE • MORE THAN THREE DECADES HAVE GONE BY since Susanne and I

embarked on the adventure that turned into the original edition of this book. It was

December 1974 when we both drove into the Hopi reservation in a rented Volkswagen

bug—me for the first time—the day after almost freezing to death watching the nighttime

proceedings of the Zuni shalakos. It was my first time in the American Southwest, and at

Zuni and then Hopi I had the odd sense that I had stepped not so much off a plane that

had flown 2,000 miles but back in time some 500 years.

The Hopis had not permitted any general photography in their villages since

shortly after the turn of the twentieth century, and it was an enormous honor for

Susanne that they had reached out to select her to produce a wide-ranging portrait of the

Hopi way. This was the original idea of Abbott Sekaquaptewa, the tribal chairman at the

time and one of the great statesmen of this country. He had seen

Susanne's earlier book, *Song of the Earth Spirit*, which portrayed the

lives of some traditional Navajo families. I later suggested to Abbott

that he probably picked Susanne because "if she could make

Navajos look that good, think what she could do with the noble Hopis." Abbott did not, in fact, deny it.

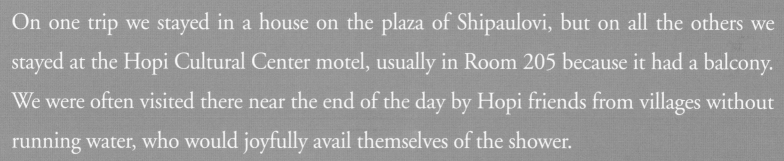

In all we made some thirty trips from Washington, D.C., to Hopi over the next eight years, some as brief as a day or two, one as long as three months. On one trip we stayed in a house on the plaza of Shipaulovi, but on all the others we stayed at the Hopi Cultural Center motel, usually in Room 205 because it had a balcony. We were often visited there near the end of the day by Hopi friends from villages without running water, who would joyfully avail themselves of the shower.

Once we had completed our work on this book and it was published in 1982, Susanne in particular was profoundly nervous about how it would be received by the Hopis. Would we be welcomed back? We had consulted with the elder Valjean Joshvema from Oraibi to make sure none of the photographs selected for the book showed anything that should not be seen, and Abbott had read the manuscript. But still, one never knows. Our bout of nerves was short-lived, thank heaven. Since 1982, we have made countless trips to Hopiland, surely more than we made before 1982, visiting what have become lifelong friends, attending (and photographing) special events such as weddings, particularly among the Sekaquaptewa family of the Eagle Clan, which took Susanne in as a kind of adoptee, and among the extended Quavehema family of Second Mesa.

Recently when Susanne was visiting Hopi, a woman came up to her and shook her hand, saying that she was happy to have been included among the pictures in the book. Susanne never forgets a face she has photographed and she was sure she had never seen this woman before. It turned out that the woman was a baby held in the arms of an adult who was standing in a crowd on the roofs around the plaza during a social dance that Susanne had been asked to photograph.

In writing the book, we changed the names of the Quavehema family out of respect for their privacy. Alonzo and Linda Quavehema were called Emory and Velma Koochwa-

tewa. Years later Alonzo told me that the name change had not been necessary and in fact had not worked. He chuckled, regaling me with stories of *pahanas* (white people) who would ask at the post office where Emory Koochwatewa lived and then turn up on his doorstep, of course calling him Emory throughout the visit…to Alonzo's ongoing amusement.

The original publisher of *Hopi*, Harry N. Abrams Publishers, kept it in print until 2005—twenty-three years, which is pretty long for a large-format photographic book. With its reissuing in a redesigned format by Rio Nuevo Publishers in 2008, we have taken the opportunity to give Alonzo and his family back their real names. On the other hand we have made no other changes in the text, while adding some other photographs taken back then. Rather than update the story in any way, we have chosen to keep it a portrait of Hopi in the 1970s. That appears to be what Abbott and others who helped us had in mind. Since then the Hopis have not let other photographers come in to do general photography. Maybe in the 2070s?

It goes without saying that our times among the Hopi people changed our lives in a profound way. Perhaps readers of this new edition of Hopi will have a similar experience. We hope so.

LYONS, COLORADO, 2008

> It was discomfiting to realize that there,
> in a place that was more ancient than any we could trace our
> forebears to, it was we who were unnecessary.

WARNING

OLD ORAIBI... On the map we could see that the village of Oraibi was located in the heart of the Hopi Indian Reservation in northeastern Arizona, about 185 miles north of Phoenix and about 230 miles west of Albuquerque. We could see that the Hopi Reservation was a lozenge-shaped area smaller than Rhode Island located amidst the far vaster, nearly New England-sized Navajo Reservation. With all the Indian reservations uniformly shaded brown, none of this meant very much to us.

We knew that Oraibi was the place that had been continuously inhabited for a longer time than any other in North America. That meant something to us, since we were, like many Americans, properly attuned to statistics.

So we drove west from the Albuquerque airport, through desert land sprinkled with iron-dark lava. Hours later we began to see the mesas rise up north of us, and we passed through the bustling, tacky cityscape of Gallup

and soon speeded into upland forests of juniper, piñon, and ponderosa pine. We plummeted down into what seemed low country (but is actually more than a mile above sea level), and after an hour or so, yellow mesas rose up around us like aged battleships frozen in a dry brown sea. It was December 1974, and outside the heated cockpit of the little rented Volkswagen the temperature was about 10 degrees Fahrenheit.

Two years earlier, Susanne had published a book, *Song of the Earth Spirit*, about the lives of some Navajo people who live north of Black Mesa, a high formation of rock some 60 by 30 miles in extent that is a major feature of the land in northeastern Arizona. At the southern tip of Black Mesa, three fingers of high cliffs extend out into the desert-like plain below, and on these three bits of high ground the Hopi located their villages a long time ago. The Hopi Tribal Chairman had seen Susanne's book about the nearby Navajo families and had decided, along with a number of religious elders and with the approval of the Tribal Council, that it was time a similar book was published about the Hopi. The two tribes do not have especially cordial relations, and perhaps the Hopi Council thought that if Susanne could make the

Hopi men do the knitting (here of black ceremonial socks) and weave the white robes and shrouds of Hopi brides. The men often make their knitting needles from the wire handles of old paint cans.

LEFT: Bertha Kinale fires her pottery out on the farthest point of the village of Walpi, high on First Mesa. Hopi potters use highly combustible sheep and cow dung to achieve the great heat required.

BELOW RIGHT: The forbidding sign outside the ancient village of Oraibi that confronted us in December 1974, suggesting that we might fail as we undertook this book.

Navajo look so dignified and tender, she could certainly show the Hopi to equal advantage. It was, in fact, a very difficult time in the history of Hopi-Navajo relations, and it is likely (though it was never discussed in detail with us) that the Hopi, who had discouraged photography among themselves on their reservation since 1910, thought the time had come for the Hopi to be represented—the way they saw themselves—in the libraries of America.

Clearly, such a call was a considerable honor, and Susanne responded immediately. She had both written and photographed the Navajo book but had found it nearly impossible to photograph and write at the same time. I was at the time an editor of *Smithsonian* magazine and was therefore enlisted to carry out the writing duties. The Hopi Tribal Chairman had said he would introduce us to some families and let matters unfold as, or if, they would.

Thus it was that we found ourselves driving past the small town of Keams Canyon and thence toward the three spurs of Black Mesa—named First, Second, and Third Mesa—past the little villages perched on the first two mesas, until we reached Third Mesa and saw on the left-hand side of the highway a green sign that told us we had reached Oraibi.

Oraibi, generally considered the seat of ancient Hopi tradition, was at the time a forlorn collection of stone buildings almost indistinguishable from the piles of boulders strewn down the sides of the mesa it sits on. Built on rock and sand and dust, perched some 600 feet above a desert that stretched to the western horizon, Oraibi was a village without electricity but one that, it seemed, had not so much turned its back on modernity as it had simply always had its vision focused on altogether different lights.

Oraibi was dark in the low winter sun, fragile but somehow ominous with age and a kind of wisdom that arose from a different world altogether—a world we hoped that with patience we would come to understand.

Then we saw the sign.

It was discomfiting to realize that there, in a place that was more ancient than any we could trace our forebears to, it was we who were unnecessary.

Long since I had stopped worrying about a little civic cheating, like speeding on Route 264 from Keams Canyon to Oraibi. We looked out of our warm little car at the sign posted outside that ancient village and felt small. What right did we have, outsiders, imagining that in the relatively brief amount of time we would be able to devote to it, we could hope to understand a society so remote and so old that it could confidently erect a sign like that?

Confronted by the sign's stern rectitude, we suddenly felt that the enterprise we had embarked upon—to understand and explain something of the Hopi way—was presumptuous, even preposterous.

Since that time in 1974, we have paid twenty-two visits to Hopi, several on behalf of the Smithsonian Institution and, more recently, the National Geographic Society. In the late 1970s the sign outside Oraibi was replaced by another—less stern but still proclaiming the village's desire for a modicum of privacy. And then, late in 1981, it was replaced by yet another, stating simply, No Non-Indians Allowed.

Considered by other Native Americans as "the oldest of the people," having lived in the same place for a millennium, the Hopi are traditionally an agricultural people, growing corn and other vegetables, as well as fruit, in the dry

WARNING   WARNING
NO OUTSIDE WHITE VISITORS
ALLOWED. BECAUSE OF YOUR
FAILURE TO OBEY THE LAWS
OF OUR TRIBE AS WELL AS THE
LAWS OF YOUR OWN, THIS
VILLAGE IS HEREBY CLOSED.

washes and sandy plains below their remote mesas. While increasingly subject to the forces of twentieth-century America, their culture is intact to a degree unique among American Indians. Its most celebrated feature is the plaza dances, two-day rituals (often attended by white friends and tourists) that are part of an elaborate year-long ceremonial cycle tying the Hopi to their land in a deeply religious manner. A scholar writing at the turn of the century termed the Hopi the most religious people in the world.

In the eight years since our first trip to Hopi we have gotten to know a host of Hopi people, observed some of their ceremonies, feasted with them, worked with them in their fields, slept in their homes, searched for eagles with them in the outlying cliffs and canyons, visited some of their shrines, made many friends among them. Yet to claim that we are experts on the Hopi way would indeed be presumptuous. What we know from being with them, and from listening to their explanations of things, are some stories about Hopi. In a sense, this book is one of discovery; it evolved as the Hopi revealed themselves to us over time, permitting us to see and to photograph some of the concerns and complexities of their lives—though, it should be said at once, not *all* the complexities by a long shot. We intuitively asked very few questions, feeling from the start that it would be best not to be inquisitive in the often intrusive manner of the journalist or social scientist. Instead we really just "hung around" and let Hopi people tell us what they wanted to tell us when they wanted to tell it. Our book, with its particular emphases (and omissions), is only as accurate a record as we can construct of what many Hopi people—though by no means all—wanted us to know about them, their lives, and their concerns. As it turned out, reticence seems to have been the right approach. We learned some six years after our first trip that our behavior had been watched by a number of religious leaders and that they, apparently finding us trustworthy, arranged for us to see and to photograph some things outsiders rarely see—or even hear about.

One of the first things we had to come to grips with, while slowly beginning to find our way around in their culture, was the split between the groups that seemed to be called, respectively, the traditionalists and the progressives. This split came into fairly clear focus for us as we grew to know one of the families to whom we were officially introduced. In the early years of our visits, this family had become embroiled in a relatively typical inter-village dispute that revealed a good deal about the nature of Hopi life, including the traditionalist-versus-progressive matter. Thus the first chapter of this book introduces Hopi life as we encountered it early on, raising questions, answering some. Subsequent chapters—on ceremony, daily life, the Hopi past, their world of spirits, and their land—double back in a sense, answering early questions, and, inevitably, leaving some unanswered.

There are some things shown in these pages that no white had ever before seen, but that is not at all what is important. There are some things shown here which most Hopi will recognize as altogether common in their lives, however exotic they may seem to an outsider. And that is not what is important either. If anything of merit arises from this volume, it will be the understanding that the Hopi have their own way, a way distinct from that of any other people, yet one that has much to offer to the rest of us…and that their way persists even as it changes and grows.

The Hopi consider a smile to be sacred.

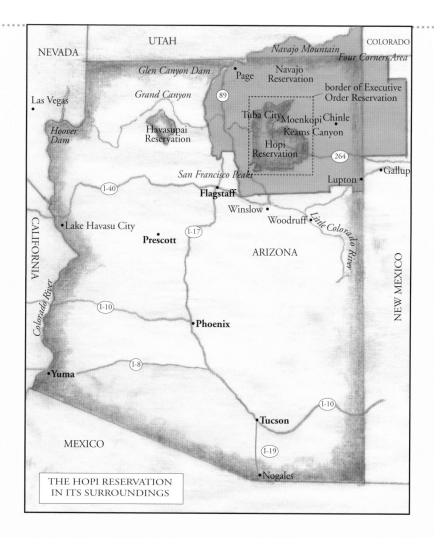

THE HOPI RESERVATION
IN ITS SURROUNDINGS

We use the word Hopi as we have heard it used: as a noun (the name of a place and of the people who live in that place), as an adjective, and as both singular and plural. Thus at Hopi we learned about some Hopi customs from various Hopi. As for Hopi terms, we have followed Hopi common practice—what one hears when Hopi words occur in English conversations among Hopi—even to forming English plurals by adding *s* at the end of Hopi words. Also we have resorted to certain circumlocutions about some religious matters so that uninitiated Hopi children would not learn from this book by accident what they should learn from their elders at an appropriate time.

The names of some of the individuals in this book have been changed to protect their privacy. All the events described occurred before our eyes or have been reliably recorded elsewhere. Our perceptions are, of course, our own, informed by no academic specialty and no personal ideology. No Hopi who has helped us in the preparation of this book—and heaven knows there is no way that all who did could be enumerated, much less adequately thanked—should be held responsible for a single word or image. We hope, nevertheless, that this book honors the Hopi in the same degree as they have honored us by letting us enjoy their friendship, good humor, and wisdom. And we have tried to pay heed to a caveat delivered to us by a Hopi friend while the manuscript was getting started—good advice for any endeavor. Try and be brief, our friend said, and tell the truth.

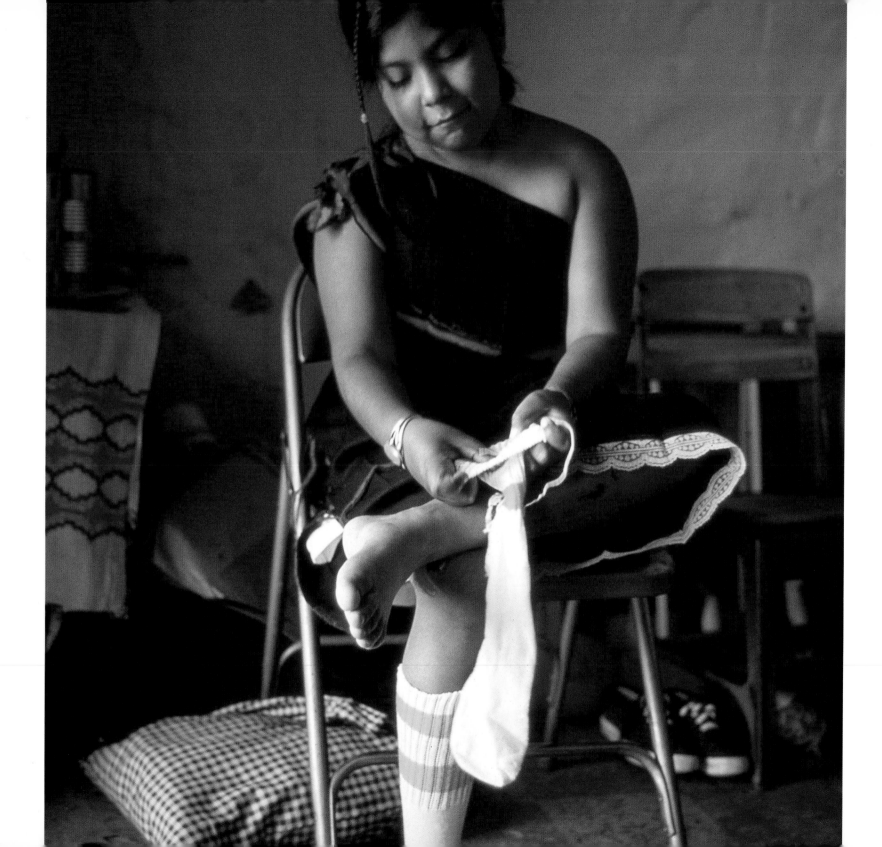

We found that whether a Hopi takes a traditional
or a progressive stand depends on what subject is being discussed,
on which mesa, in which village, and with which clan.

TRADITIONAL vs. PROGRESSIVE

HOPI MEANS "the peaceful people," it is said. Indeed, it is true that throughout their long history of living on the remote mesas of northeastern Arizona, they have sought to avoid violence and bloodshed. Yet anyone who spends much time among the Hopi knows that they tend to be fractious and are in nearly perpetual argument among themselves about which of them is living a truly proper Hopi life. A Hopi leader has written: "The term 'peaceful people' was a definition some white man came up with. It is only one of the meanings of Hopi. The profound meaning of the word is 'righteous.' We don't use that very much because it sounds too much like 'self-righteous,' which I have heard many elders say describes one of our big shortcomings as a people. The closest contemporary explanation is 'virtuous,' meaning good, moral, of good behavior. That is my opinion."

Preparing for a dance in her native village of Shipaulovi, a girl wears a traditional Hopi dress, a *manta*. Before donning buckskin leggings and moccasins, she pulls on a pair of athletic socks—reflecting the mixture of old and new in contemporary Hopi life.

In our first week at Hopi, in December 1974, Susanne and I spent time with two Hopi families, both of whom illustrated not only the striving to be good but also the disputatiousness of Hopi life. One was the family of Thomas Banyacya, who calls himself a "traditionalist." The other was the family of Alonzo Quavehema, whom Thomas calls a "progressive." Thomas lived in one of the four villages of Third Mesa, the westernmost of the three Hopi mesas. Alonzo lived in one of the three villages of Second Mesa.

We had become acquainted with Thomas several months before our first trip to Hopi, having met him on the street in Washington, D.C., by chance—if indeed there is such a thing as chance. He had been attending a conservation conference. People who have any association with the Hopi usually meet Thomas first, for Thomas is a very public man, a man with a mission. He spent a couple of nights in our house at our invitation, and one night he told us of his mission. He was, he said, the official interpreter for the traditional leaders of the Independent Hopi Nation. There never had been a treaty signed between the United States and the Hopi, and its elders,

he explained, still considered Hopi a nation unto itself. That evening Thomas took out a piece of cloth and spread it over his knees. On it he had stitched an elaborate design, copied from a sacred rock carving located near Oraibi. It was a symbolic representation of the Hopi creation story and of the Hopi prophecies. Using the cloth as a kind of mnemonic device, Thomas outlined how the Hopi had emerged long ago from the Underworld and entered this world, how they had split up into various groups and roamed the earth, predestined to regroup in the Four Corners area of the American Southwest (where Arizona, New Mexico, Utah, and Colorado join)—the gathering of the clans. Thomas explained how the Hopi prophecies foretold that all the various clans would eventually settle on the present Hopi mesas and practice their religion in harmony with the desert land, which in turn would be fruitful and benevolent.

He went on to say that with the arrival of the white man (in Hopi, *pahana*) it became clear that the Hopi way would be attacked—both subtly and brutally. Hopi land would be taken away. The prophecies foretold this also.

In the mid-1940s, shortly after World War II, the traditionalist elders got together to review, and apparently revise, the prophecies. Some of the elders, Thomas reported, said their grandfathers had spoken of highways in the sky (airplanes) and a fiery gourd (nuclear weapon) long before such things had been invented. The prophecies were enunciated again, including the certainty that the old Hopi ways were being eroded according to schedule and that the world would soon erupt in mass destruction, the only survivors to be those Hopi who had steadfastly followed the true path. At the time of the meeting, the elders had appointed Thomas to be their spokesman, and ever since he had traveled the country trying to enlist the aid of others to help the Hopi traditionalists, against the odds even of their prophecies, to avert the twin catastrophes of the erosion of Hopi values and mass destruction.

The white man's civilization spelled doom for the Hopi way, according to Thomas, because the cash economy of the white man—the need to have money to pay for modern appliances, for example—would force Hopi to take jobs, and this would distract them from the spiritual values embodied in the traditional agricultural life and the yearly ceremonial cycle that was inextricably tied to the hard life of the Hopi farmer. But Hopi history and prophecy also held that a white man, a particular individual called the White Brother, had emerged from the Underworld at the time of the Hopi arrival here and had gone east. He would one day return and bring aid to the beleaguered Hopi.

Thomas said that he was glad we had been asked to undertake a book about the tribe but that we should be extremely wary of the Tribal Council. It was the Council, he said, that had been persuaded by a Mormon law firm from Salt Lake City and by the great corporations to sell out their rights to the land to the mineral interests. The Tribal Council itself, he said, was full of Mormonized Hopi, not true Hopi, and was, as a government entity, illegal, having been forced down the throats of the traditional Hopi by the U.S. government back in the 1930s. The traditionalist elders, Thomas said, had asked him to travel the world, explaining the dire situation and seeking help. Through his intervention, for example, the elders had allied themselves with local environmental groups in the early 1970s to try and block the Peabody Coal Company from strip-mining the northern end of Black Mesa—a sacred place. He had even gone to the United

Nations Conference on the Human Environment in Stockholm in June 1972 to press the Hopi case. The elders had made him a passport out of parchment and eagle feathers, which had attracted considerable attention at the conference. Thomas invited us to stay with him when we came to Hopi in December. We were now forewarned that we would encounter both heroes and villains there.

•

After our dismaying encounter with the sign at Oraibi, we drove down off the mesa and turned into the village of New Oraibi, now called Kykotsmovi—to look for Thomas's house. Kykotsmovi is a relatively new village, having been settled after the turn of the century, with yellow stone houses sprinkled here and there on either side of a single paved road. Among these one-story buildings were some frame houses, a few churches, and, at the far end of town, the office building that housed the tribal administration. Nestled in a low area near the post office, a small cinder-block building with an American flag fluttering bravely above it, we found Thomas's house, or rather houses. One rectangular building of stone was joined to an older, smaller stone structure. Outside, a couple of old cars were on blocks. Thomas's wife, Fermina—a small woman in her fifties, wearing an apron—answered our knock. She said that Thomas was away on business. He would be back in two days, but we were welcome to stay with her: she had been expecting us.

In the house was a small kitchen with the usual equipment—a sink, a gas stove, and an electric refrigerator. Just off the kitchen was a living room, which was cluttered with furniture, an electric organ, and a small Christmas tree.

Down a hall were bedrooms and a bathroom. Fermina instructed us to put our things in the nearest bedroom and served us dinner. (It turned out that it was her bedroom; she slept on the sofa in the living room while we were there.)

The next day we discovered that the Tribal Chairman was also away for two days. We spent most of the next two days rather aimlessly driving around the mesas, engaging in an activity of paramount importance at Hopi: waiting. The night of the second day, Thomas returned, exhausted, from his travels. He was glad to see us, he said, but we could tell that he was too tired for any conversation, so we went to bed.

The next morning Thomas seemed agitated. He bundled us into his pickup truck and drove to the village of Shungopavi on Second Mesa. Along the way he explained briefly that there was to be a meeting of the traditionalist elders and the lawyers they had retained. The problem was housing. Some people in Shipaulovi, another village on Second Mesa, had, with the aid of the Tribal Council, obtained money from the U.S. Department of Housing and Urban Development (HUD) and were planning to build some new houses down on the desert floor below the village. Thomas said that because the land selected for the houses was not only sacred land but belonged to Shungopavi, not Shipaulovi, the traditionalist leaders of Shungopavi and other villages were seeking to block the project. The matter was urgent, since the plans were very far along. This was another example, Thomas pointed out, of how the Tribal Council was interfering with the traditional authority of the elders and rending the fabric of Hopi life.

We stopped at the far end of the village of Shungopavi, near the mesa edge, and Thomas led us through a side door into a *kiva* (a mostly underground

LEFT: Behind the plaza at Walpi, a ladder rises through the roof of a kiva.

RIGHT: Abbott Sekaquaptewa, of the Eagle Clan, was the elected chairman of the Hopi Tribal Council until 1981. An indefatigable struggler for the dignity of the Hopi people and the continuance of their traditional ways, this distinguished leader—a true statesman—is a skilled interpreter in Hopi, English, and Navajo.

rectangular room used as a meeting place as well as for ceremonial occasions). It had stucco walls and great round beams supporting poles that ran lengthwise along the ceiling, holding up the mud and thatch of the roof. A ladder made of poles lashed together extended down at an angle through a square hole in the ceiling. A bar of sunlight beamed through the hole, at a different angle. Several old men sat on stools in the center of the room, smoking pipes and cigarettes and spitting into the sand around an ancient coal stove. They were small men with leathery, wrinkled faces; most of them wore colorful scarves folded into bands wrapped around their foreheads. A few others sat on benches around the walls, along with two white men in business suits, the traditionalists' lawyers, members of a Phoenix law firm. Other elders arrived, descending the ladder. The beam of sunlight filled up with curls of smoke. In due course, Thomas spoke—in Hopi— then turned to us and said that he had explained who we were and asked that I take notes. The proceedings then began. One of the elders stood up and began talking in Hopi; an interpreter translated for the benefit of the lawyers, and us.

"Who came here first?" asked the elder.

"The Hopi came first," replied the older of the two lawyers, a big, blustery former State Supreme Court justice with a mane of white hair and an air of the old frontier about him.

The elder proceeded to recount Hopi history and prophecies, explaining how the sacred clan lands came to be, and how the white man and his "puppy," the Tribal Council, were fulfilling the prophecies by destroying those lands.

The white-maned lawyer agreed, saying that big corporations were trying to whip the Hopi with money, buying the allegiance of the young people. He argued against litigation, however, suggesting that the big corporations and the law firm retained by the Tribal Council would tie the matter up for years and wear the traditionalists down. He said that it was essential for the Hopi to preserve their religion "down through the aisles of history," and suggested that they all meet with the Council and seek a fair compromise.

There were objections to this on the grounds that a formal meeting with the Council would constitute legal recognition of that body. It was clear to all present that the main issue in this and all other disputes was the authority of the religious elders versus the authority of the Tribal Council. The lawyers understood that in the past the traditionalists had lost power and they pledged to get it back for them. They would themselves go to the Council and explain that the individual who had signed the paper permitting the leasing of the lands below Shipaulovi was not authorized to do so in the eyes of the elders. The lawyers asked if there was a map of the sacred land. There was not; these things were known by the elders, by markers, by knowledge passed down through generations. They suggested that a map be drawn. The meeting came to an end, and the lawyers left to arrange a meeting with the Tribal Chairman.

That afternoon Susanne and I visited the Tribal Chairman, Abbott Sekaquaptewa. Abbott explained that though the Tribal Council had indeed authorized him to invite us to begin work on a book about the Hopi, we should be aware that most Hopi people were extremely reluctant to be photographed, if not actually opposed to it; that most of the villages, as we no doubt had already noticed, had signs on their outskirts forbidding photography; and that there were many things that we could not photograph under any circumstances,

among them the ceremonies for which the Hopi are most famous—the kachina dances. He would introduce us to a man named Alonzo Quavehema who lived in Shipaulovi; Alonzo had discussed our project with Abbott and had agreed to act as a kind of guide. He had been on the Tribal Council for several years but was also highly regarded by the traditionalist elders.

Thus it was that two days later we stood on the edge of the turret-like mesa that bears the stone and cinder-block houses of Shipaulovi, talking to Alonzo Quavehema, feeling embroiled in a dispute we did not understand, in a culture we knew practically nothing about. Not only had Alonzo served on the Tribal Council, which made him a progressive by definition, but also, it turned out, he had been on the Hopi Housing Committee that had organized and planned the controversial housing to which the traditionalists were so opposed.

Alonzo was a quiet, affable man in his early forties, with smile lines around his eyes. He had a ready grin and a pleasant, somewhat nasal lilt to his voice. Without saying much at first, he made us feel not only welcome but important. He concentrated his attention on us—not so much to inquire about us and our purposes as, it seemed, to convince us that we would learn from moment to moment what we needed to understand. During eight years of visiting him and his family we would come to realize that Alonzo is, simply, one of the best men (in the sense of striving to be good) we have ever known. We would learn also that he is held in high esteem among Hopi elders, not only for his assiduousness in performing his traditional Hopi obligations but also because he is one of the supreme composers of the songs that the Hopi kachinas sing during ceremonies (he never told us he was a poet). It is really good to know that there is yet a society among us that considers poets essential. The meaning of our experience among the Hopi is the realization that affection and love can precede under-standing—that, in fact, there is no such thing as total understanding across cul-tures. To seek patterns of behavior in such situations, and describe them in such a way that other scholars can make close comparisons—that is science. We chose, instead, to hope we would make friends. Alonzo and his family, and Abbott and others, became better friends than we could—in 1974—have imag-ined was possible. But still we speak a different language. What we know now of Hopi is what we learned over time. It starts, truly, with what Alonzo told us that first day about his clan.

Looking out across the desert some 600 feet below him to the western spur of Second Mesa, jutting out into the scrub like a fortress a mile and a half away, Alonzo explained how it had come to be that he lived here in the village of Shipaulovi. Scattered over the distant mesa-top were some houses and a water tower glinting in the late afternoon sun. That was the village of Shungopavi, where we had met with Thomas and the lawyers.

"My people went over there first, to Shungopavi. We came up from the south, near Winslow, and asked the leaders of Shungopavi if we could live there. We told them all the things we could do to help. We were warriors. We could be their guards. They couldn't decide for a long time if we could join their village.

"Finally they decided that Shungopavi was too crowded, so they told us we could come over here and start a village. They said they would send a Bear Clan family with us to be our leaders. The Bear Clan is traditionally the clan of the Hopi leaders.

"So we came over to this mesa one day, and as we arrived the sun was coming up—just showing its forehead, you know. So they named us the Sun Forehead Clan."

These events, which Alonzo was recounting with the familiarity of a participant, had taken place about 600 years ago, by his estimate. Alonzo's people were, it seemed, late arrivals on the Hopi mesas. The Hopi are a collection of people who over a period of hundreds of years, beginning about a millennium ago, gathered on the mesas after many years of journeying about the region. The first to arrive were the people of the Bear Clan; they were followed soon after by a number of other groups, which became individual clans like the Bluebird

Clan and the Bear Strap Clan. Each newly arriving group had to persuade the Bear Clan people that they had some special ceremony, some talent, some particular way of intervening in the natural scheme of things, that would be helpful to the gathering Hopi people. Some brought with them, Hopi history says, magical talents for making rain; others brought more tangible assets such as the warrior status of Alonzo's forebears. The Snake Clan arrived with a special talent for manipulating the spirits of the snakes to act as messengers to the gods that bring rain, and they were accepted into the Hopi world for that reason.

Currently there are some thirty clans among the Hopi. Many have died out, in some cases their functions having been passed on to other clans, in other cases their functions having died out with them. In a society of 10,000 people, which in earlier times was generally in the range of 2,000 to 3,000 people, and in which clanship is inherited through the mother, it is not difficult to imagine that a small clan could disappear in one generation of few or no daughters. Except for those among us who hark back to Scotland for our roots, there is no comparable concept of the clan in most non-Indian American society, and it is extremely difficult to conceive of what clan relationship means among the Hopi. We sometimes speak of our extended family—uncles and aunts, grandparents, cousins, and so forth—as our clan. Among the Hopi, clan denotes far more than that. Clan locates a Hopi in a large social world, all parts of which are interconnected. A child born into a household knows its mother's sisters (some of whom are in fact her cousins) as mothers, and all their offspring as brothers and sisters. The child also knows all its "mothers'" brothers as uncles. All members of the father's clan are additional kin. And there are constellations

of clans (called by anthropologists "phratries"). The Bear Clan, for example, from which the leaders arise, is closely allied to a handful of other clans, such as the Bluebird Clan and the Bear Strap Clan. One does not marry a member of one's own clan. Indeed, one does not marry a member of an associated clan (but this tradition is apparently breaking down).

Thus the clans constitute a system whereby the gene pool is kept relatively free of inbreeding. In addition, the clans provide each Hopi with a vast number of relatives. With each relationship there is a prescribed series of obligations. Uncles, for example, have the right and duty to discipline youthful members of the clan.

We were altogether baffled by the apparently endless number of sisters Linda introduced us to until she explained that they all belonged to the Tobacco Clan—or the associated Rabbit Clan. "We are almost all related, one way or another," said Linda. The clan system, seemingly in a state of perpetual if slow evolution, is indeed one of the main forms of social glue that has historically held the separate Hopi villages together. For until well into this century there was no particular tribal government among the Hopi, only a loose confederation of politically independent villages, rather like the city-states of ancient Greece, knit together by basically similar views of their history, by similar religious beliefs and ceremonial practices, and by web within web of kinship based not only on blood but also, and to a greater extent, on clan. Thus on our first meeting with Alonzo, he sought to make clear the history of his clan, and the working of the clan system. First things first…then he began to talk of himself.

Almost his entire life had been spent within the area defined in the executive order by which President Chester A. Arthur had established the Hopi Indian Reservation in 1882. He had four years of high school in Albuquerque, a stint in the army in Korea and Japan, and a few youthful trips to Chicago with a troupe of Hopi dancers. He was now employed as a cook in a day school in the Third Mesa village of Kykotsmovi. In the early 1970s, he and his family had lived in a two-room house on Shipaulovi's plaza, a dusty rectangle 36 by 15 paces, surrounded by one-story houses. Five other similarly quartered families lived around the plaza, where, on ceremonial days, dances are held and where more than a thousand people may congregate, sitting in chairs around the plaza and lining the rooftops three or four deep. On ordinary days the plaza is relatively quiet. The adults stay inside most of the time, doing chores and avoiding the outdoor heat or cold. The sound of chanting is heard: the songs and sounds of Hopi dances that have been tape-recorded and are played throughout the day. Small troops of children appear, disappear, and reappear, playing in the dusty square.

Alonzo's house, with foot-thick walls of native stone and large round pine beams holding up a roof with earth piled on it for insulation, had electricity but no running water. Twice a week Alonzo would get water for drinking, washing, and cooking from a windmill-driven pump five miles away in the desert below and haul it up the mesa in fifty-gallon drums in the back of his wheezing pickup. From the truck it would be transferred, bucket by bucket, into a galvanized can in the kitchen. Since the Cal Gas truck could not make it around the last precipitous switchback on the road that winds its way up to Shipaulovi, Alonzo would also haul 200-pound propane bottles up the mesa from sixteen miles away. In the winter he burned coal that he collected free from the Peabody Coal Company mine on Black Mesa—a five-hour round trip. A cluster of

Many of the villages are without running water. At Shipaulovi Linda Quavehema's son Phillip hauls water in buckets from a fifty-gallon drum he filled five miles away at a windmill.

outhouses were perched in the rocks thirty feet down the side of the mesa from the back door. Not a particularly convenient way to live.

However, for Alonzo and Linda the true Hopi way does not require the deliberate eschewing of modern conveniences or modern trappings. On our first visit to their house, before we stepped outside with Alonzo to look over the desert to Shungopavi, we watched a professional football game on television while Linda and her daughter Jan wove plaques—round, basket-like trays made of coiled yucca leaves—in the traditional way.

Before we met them, Linda and Alonzo had lived briefly in a sixty-foot trailer below the mesa on some desert land given to Linda by her grandfather, whom she had cared for during the last eleven years of his life. There life was easier; they enjoyed the convenience of running water, for example, as only those who have lived without it for a period of time can. "The kids got used to taking showers every day, sometimes twice a day," Alonzo told us good-humoredly. There was more room for them to play, and they were able to go bicycling—which was rather dangerous on the top of the mesa. It was easier to get to school; the school bus didn't venture up to the top of the mesa any more than the Cal Gas truck did. Yet the family remained connected to the village on top. During the ceremonial days, chiefly between January and August, they would spend Thursdays to Sundays in their old house in Shipaulovi, preparing for and taking part in the ceremonies. "I went up there every day," said Alonzo, "just to see what was going on."

But living "down below" had had some disadvantages. Some people said that it was too much like living the white man's way; it was controversial, and

A Navajo Dance, this one held in the village of Shipaulovi, takes a great deal of practice and preparation. The boys and girls are painstakingly adorned by their uncles, aunts, and parents. When they are ready, all the dancers form up in an area outside the plaza and, at the signal of the village man who is sponsoring the dance, file into the plaza. The dance will last about half an hour and, after a rest period, it will be repeated over and over again, for two days in August.

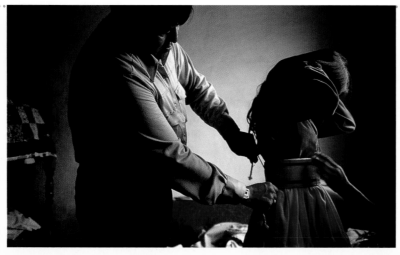

controversy is not good. In any case, it did not last long. A particularly strong wind blew the roof off the trailer, and the family moved back up on top to their little house on the plaza. They were resolved, nonetheless, to save enough money to one day build a proper house on Linda's land on the desert floor.

Alonzo walked around to the other side of the mesa and looked at the desert below to the east and toward the village on top of First Mesa, a narrow blade of land that thrust out at us some six miles away. Alonzo pointed out the sandy patches on the desert floor that were cornfields and peach orchards. He recalled that when he was a boy the entire valley had seemed to be green in summer with fields and orchards.

The weather had been better in those times, though. He wondered if the climate had changed throughout the United States. But he suspected that the bad weather they had experienced during the past two years was caused not so much by climate change as by something far deeper—a breakdown in the traditional Hopi way, in this instance the result of the housing dispute between his village, Shipaulovi, and Shungopavi, and the bad thoughts people were harboring as a result.

The village of Shipaulovi was growing, Alonzo explained; there was no more room on the mesa for the additional houses needed as its population rose above 200. The plan was to build twenty-one houses on a strip of land below the mesa along the road to Winslow. The strip of land was to be leased from the village of Shipaulovi but, as we already knew, Shungopavi, on the western spur of Second Mesa, also claimed the land.

"This isn't a dispute between the Tribal Council and the traditionalists," Alonzo said. "It's a dispute between the two villages. I know what the traditionalists are worried about. They believe if we build those houses down there like pahana houses, then we'll become pahanas. We'll lose our Hopi ways. And those are all we have, our old ways. Here at Shipaulovi we try to keep the old ways, we perform all the ceremonies, the dances. At Oraibi and some other villages, they don't do most of the dances anymore. It's hard to know where it will all end."

In May 1975, when we returned to the reservation, Alonzo said the housing problem was now settled, and the water pipes were being laid. The Quavehemas were caught up in the daily round of traditional activity. It was the height of the ceremonial cycle, and it was time to plant crops. They were busy fulfilling the many obligations to relatives and neighbors that Hopi tradition has dictated for centuries. For Hopi is a society in which not only is virtually everyone related but most of one's life is bound up in a web of mutual obligations—almost in a ritual sense. For example, the plaques Linda was making while Alonzo and I

After the dancers have performed, they leave the plaza for a rest, a chat, or some refreshment. Some may abandon their cumbersome headgear at the nearby kiva. Often—usually by the second day—another village will send a group of dancers in a show of support for the host village, and the two groups will alternate in the plaza.

watched television on our first visit to their house in December 1974 had to do with what the Hopi call social dances but are really occasions—usually lasting two days—when young people, male and female, carry out ceremonies in the village plazas. A number of these ceremonial events, for example the Navajo Dance, celebrate other tribes; another kind is the Buffalo Dance, which is traditionally held in February. These are highly repetitive, ritualized performances and they have religious significance, but not to the same degree as the ceremonies for which the Hopi are most widely known—those solemn events in which the kachinas, Hopi deities, dance in the plazas for two days at a time petitioning for rain for the crops. Organizing and carrying out any one of these ceremonies, or social dances, calls for a tremendous amount of teamwork, and the participants and their relatives incur a host of obligations. A girl who participates in a social dance incurs an obligation to her partners' families, and these debts often pile up. The plaques Linda was making were to "pay back" the families of boys who had danced with her twelve-year-old daughter, Darlene.

From April to June there is a kachina dance in one or another village just about every weekend—all tied to the planting and growing season. On the day when we returned in May 1975, such a dance was taking place in Shipaulovi. In the course of the day sixty people—friends, clan members, and relatives—trooped through the house and sat down at the kitchen table to be fed the Hopi stew called *noqkwivi* (a combination of hominy and mutton), bread, and coffee. It is considered rude not to visit a related family when there is a ceremony in that family's village, ruder still not to sit down at the table and eat. One can wind up eating eight meals a day on these occasions.

Alonzo was taking part in the ceremony, which meant not only the two exhausting days of the dance but many days in the kiva—rehearsing, making ceremonial paraphernalia, and fasting—as well as spending the entire night before the dance in prayer and spiritual preparation for the ceremony.

In the course of the spring and summer, Alonzo took part in six or seven such ceremonies in his and other villages, and he and Linda organized the wedding of their elder daughter, Jan. This entailed the preparation of vast quantities of food, with the help of neighbors, in order to pay back the groom's family, who, in accordance with tradition, provided the bridal robes.

The ceremonies held in the spring and summer are to bring rain, to encourage the crops. The day after the ceremony we attended in May, Alonzo took a handful of spruce branches that the kachinas had worn in the dance and had left behind in the plaza down to a dusty dry wash east of the mesa, where he had recently planted his spring corn. Normally the spring corn was planted in early April. But the cold season had lasted longer than usual, so the planting had been late and Alonzo was not sanguine.

Little green shoots, about four paces apart and protected from the wind and from cutworms by rusty tin cans placed over them, dotted the sand. Alonzo laid the spruce branches next to one of his plants, where earlier he had placed some eagle feathers, and knelt to pray. Then he began to hoe the few weeds that had managed to take hold in the sand.

"It's too bad to kill even the weeds," said Alonzo, expressing the Hopi respect for the spirit in all living things, "but they use up the moisture."

"What moisture?" I asked, looking around the expanse of dry sand.

Alonzo stuck his hoe six inches into the sand and turned it over. "There," he said, "you can see the sand is a little moist."

All I could see was dry sand.

"It's there," he assured me, laughing.

Alonzo has four such fields which he tends before and after work at the school and in between ceremonies. In separate fields, or sections of fields, he grows the traditional kinds of Hopi corn: yellow, blue, white, red, purple, and sweet. The colors signify the Hopi cardinal directions: yellow is northwest, blue southwest, white northeast, and red southeast. (These are the four directions from which the Hopi clans gathered long ago in their present land, and they also correspond with the position of the rising and setting sun during the solstices.) The purple corn represents straight up and the sweet corn (and speckled corn) down, toward the center of the earth.

Along with corn, Alonzo raises melons, gourds, and beans. But corn is the true traditional measure of Hopi wealth, and its ceremonial use is very important. A Hopi woman needs great amounts of com, for paying back and for feeding her family and relatives. One evening Linda finished shelling seventy-five pounds of blue corn, knocking the kernels off, cob by cob, by hammering them with a dry cob. By nightfall her hands were sore and throbbing, but she kept on into the night until she was done, since the corn had to be ground into meal before the weekend in order to help a neighbor pay back her daughter's in-laws in another village.

Using Linda's blue cornmeal, the neighbor would spend the better part of two days making *piki* bread, a traditional form in which blue corn is prepared.

Sitting in the small, dark piki house, a Hopi woman makes a thin gruel of water and blue cornmeal, adding a pinch of ashes to the mixture. She spreads the gruel over a flat, smooth rock placed directly above a fire. Almost instantaneously the thin layer of gruel turns into what looks like a rumpled sheet of tissue paper. This she picks up from the stone and sets aside. As she starts the next piece of piki on the stone, she takes the previous one and puts it briefly on top of the newly cooking batter, where it becomes limp. She then folds it in half and rolls it up and sets it aside. An astonishing amount of piki is given out on special occasions, and the women develop heavily calloused and occasionally blistered hands during its preparation.

"Here at Shipaulovi," Linda explained as she shelled the blue corn, "we ladies all help each other, pretty much. We all know who helps and who doesn't. A couple of ladies here don't ever help. I don't know what they're going to do if their daughters marry Hopi men. They can't do it all by themselves."

The pile of corncobs at her feet was the last of Linda's blue corn from the previous year's crop. "I sure hope we get some more this year," she said as she sat in her living room banging corncobs together under the single naked light bulb that hung from the ceiling. Alonzo frowned. Two years ago the crop had been good, but the year before it had suffered from too little rain. This year the cold weather was late departing, and shortly after the shoots had emerged, an untimely rain had flooded the corn temporarily, rotting some of it. It was in July and August that they needed the rain.

In August when we returned to the reservation it did rain, often—tantalizing brief showers here and there, but rarely on the cornfields of Shipaulovi.

BELOW: A Hopi woman from Moenkopi, a village north of the Hopi mesas, makes piki from blue corn. A mixture of blue cornmeal, water, and saltbush ashes is spread over a hot rock that has been polished smooth with crushed watermelon seeds. The paper-thin bread is then folded and rolled for storage. Eventually it is passed out in prodigious quantities at important occasions. Most daily activities are closely related to the religious and ritual life of the Hopi.

RIGHT: A Hopi stonemason and (*far right*) a sheepherder and snake priest who was one of the last of the tribe to travel by burro.

Every afternoon big, fleecy cumulus clouds would congregate on the horizon and then turn gray. Somewhere, out on the horizon, a dark ribbon of rain would connect the sky to the earth like a slow-motion bolt of lightning. And wherever it rained, the clouds would soon part and the sun would come out and dry the land so quickly that within half an hour all that was left were a few puddles along the roadsides and a faint smell of moisture in the air.

Alonzo continued to think the bad weather was connected to the housing dispute, which had erupted again. We arrived to find him exhausted from two days and two nights in a historic meeting. It was historic, the Hopi weekly newspaper *Qua Tokti* (*Cry of the Eagle*) reported, because it was the first time the traditionalists had recognized the authority of the Tribal Council to arbitrate matters in dispute between two villages.

Early that month, the village of Shungopavi had formally and in writing complained to the Council about the projected construction of houses for Shipaulovi, financed by HUD, on land below the mesa. They had hired a new lawyer, one from the Native American Rights Fund, an Indian but not a Hopi. Under the bylaws of the Hopi Constitution, the Council had to hold hearings within eight days. The proponents in Shipaulovi of the housing project immediately retained their own lawyer, a Hopi, to represent them at the hearings.

There was a disagreement about the exact location of the boundaries of the land in question. Designating it as sacred, the plaintiffs, under cross-examination, were nevertheless unable to point out on a map exactly where it was. The witness explained that the Bear Strap Clan in Shungopavi had won title to the land long ago in a fight between one of its members and a member of the Bear Clan.

On the second day of the hearings, the Council and all the witnesses adjourned and went out to the desert to determine exactly what piece of land each side was talking about. As they were setting out from the Tribal Council Hall, a man named David James was doing his laundry with his wife in a small Laundromat near Kykotsmovi on Route 264. Someone came in and told him that the Council was discussing the land dispute and suggested that he go to the meeting. David, in his late sixties, was an elder of the Bluebird Clan in Shungopavi, the clan ultimately responsible for Hopi history. Alonzo later described him to me as "a man who knows things." David went along to the housing site, to aid in finding the boundary markers in question. Three were found promptly, but the Bear Strap Clan people couldn't locate the fourth. David finally showed them where it was. The meeting resumed at the Tribal Council Hall, and David testified in behalf of Shipaulovi and the housing project. He told the Bear Strap Clan plaintiff that he had the story wrong. The plaintiff said that he had told it as his uncle had told it to him. David replied, "Well, my uncle told me that your uncle didn't know nothing."

The true story, he went on, was that two men from the two clans had coveted the land and finally decided to fight a duel over it. While clan members looked on, they stood back-to-back on the land, walked four paces, then turned and shot arrows at each other. Both were struck dead. The land was sullied by their blood soaking into it, so the people buried the two antagonists right there, with a sharp rock between them. It was declared that neither of the two clans could ever again claim the use of that land, that if anyone from the Bear Clan or the Bear Strap Clan tried to claim it, they would be

beheaded by the sharp rock. ("Not beheaded in real life," Alonzo explained, "but that is the meaning of it.")

Thus the meeting ended, with the two lawyers directed to deliver summaries to the Council, which would decide the matter within a month.

Alonzo, tired from the meetings, tired from the endless round of ceremonies, tired from work at the school and from tending his fields and hauling drums of water and bottles of propane, was an angry man in August, but he would not ascribe evil motives to his opponents: they were stirred up, misled, by outsiders.

"I know that is Shipaulovi land," said Alonzo. "Our uncles told it was there for us to live on when we became too many for the village. It has always been the place where we would expand. All these ceremonies I take part in, all our prayers…I do this partly to keep the promise of our uncles, to make sure we deserve what they have left us. We have always planned on it. The traditionalists, they want to delay it. They delayed it in 1971 and the money went to Polacca, down the road on First Mesa. Then we started again. We planned for twenty-one houses, but the delay has been so long that we can only build fourteen houses, because of inflation. I don't know what they want, the traditionalists. They are stirred up by outsiders—pahanas, Christians. Maybe that is why they do this."

A few days later we sat on Alonzo's back step and watched the full moon rise over a distant mesa, making its way up the sky past a fish-shaped gray cloud. Alonzo was about to leave for Shungopavi, where there would be a practice session for a Flute Dance (a ceremony in behalf of the spirits of those who have died in the past year). Alonzo's father had always participated in the Flute Dance in Shungopavi and Alonzo did so now that his father was dead. One of

Helen Sekaquaptewa (in sunlight) and family members shuck corn at her ranch out on the desert near Howell Mesa, in preparation for a family feast.

the participants in the practice session was to be the primary plaintiff in the housing dispute. I asked Alonzo if there would be any awkwardness in spending the night at close quarters with so bitter an opponent.

"Oh no," Alonzo said, surprised by the implication of my question. "The ceremony is too important. We stay up and sing the sacred songs all night to purify ourselves so that our prayers can do good for everyone."

At dawn, after the all-night session, we picked Alonzo up in Shungopavi and drove him home.

"The night went so fast!" he said. "Before I knew it, it was five o'clock. We didn't have time to get through all the songs. Some of those old men," he went on with admiration, "some of those old men know a whole lot of songs."

On September 5, the Hopi Tribal Council decided that the land belonged to Shipaulovi. The wrenching strife was over, at least for the time being. Alonzo and the other Hopi could turn now to other important matters. In November the eight-day Wuwutsim ceremony would take place, and at winter solstice the six-month cycle of kachina ceremonies would begin again. There were prayer feathers to make, there was corn to harvest.

•

We were puzzled—not so much by the housing dispute as by the distinction, which grew ever fuzzier in our minds, between the traditionalists and people like Alonzo. The traditionalists had what seemed an extremely plausible case. They claimed they were simply trying to keep Hopi pure and unpolluted by white culture, to save sacred lands. Had not the traditionalists, with Thomas Banyacya as

their spokesman, been the group that had made the Hopi case public when the Peabody Coal Company began to strip-mine the sacred lands north on Black Mesa? Had they not joined with various environmental groups—a rare combination—to try to fight off the ravaging of the land by this giant corporation? Were they not the true religious leaders of Hopi? Was it not noble, if slightly quixotic, to defy the dominant culture and hew to the old ways?

But a number of contradictions had begun to appear in the traditionalists' approach that worried us. How was it that Thomas Banyacya had electricity, appliances, running water, a toilet, an electric organ, and a Christmas tree in his house? How was it that Thomas and his wife sent their granddaughter, who lived with them, to a Mennonite school? Why did Thomas's wife complain that only progressive young people, and not her traditionalist children, could get jobs with the tribal administration? We heard from other Hopi about traditionalists who had opposed the installation of water lines in Shungopavi but as soon as the water was installed had come out at night to fill their buckets.

We learned that the Tribal Council was not made up of Mormonized Hopi, as Thomas Banyacya had told us, that the Tribal Chairman, Abbott Sekaquaptewa, was not a Mormon (though his mother is). Indeed, we found that some of the most respected religious leaders in all Hopi serve on the Council, and many others cooperate fully with it, providing it with guidance and support. We came to find, rather early, that there is a broad spectrum of opinion ranging from the rare highly progressive Hopi, who is ready to abandon most of his traditions, through a variety of traditionally minded people who at the same time support the Tribal Council, to traditionalists like Thomas Banyacya who appear to oppose all innovation.

BELOW RIGHT: Alonzo Quavehema visiting his field at dawn, before he goes off to his job, sprinkles sacred cornmeal on it, feeding the spirits and entreating the corn to grow. Then he puts in some time hoeing the weeds that spring up here and there, lest they rob the sandy soil below of priceless moisture.

RIGHT: Alph Secakuku, head of the Hopi office of the Bureau of Indian Affairs, strikes an enthusiastic pose on an outcrop called the Devil's Chair on the desert below Second Mesa.

What is more, we found that whether a Hopi takes a traditional or a progressive stand depends on what subject is being discussed, on which mesa, in which village, and with which clan. To an outsider it is baffling and unpredictable. The one constant appears to be that the traditionalists—many other Hopi refer to them as the "so-called traditionalists" or the "political traditionalists"—can be counted on to oppose the Tribal Council. All in all, there are about 300, perhaps 400, in this hard-core group out of a population of 10,000.

However, a great many people know the Hopi today through the intercession of these highly publicity-conscious traditionalists and see Hopi through their particular ideological lens. The political impetus behind their actions is simple: they believe that the Tribal Council was imposed upon the Hopi by the U.S. government through a constitutional referendum in which those opposed stayed home. They claim that a majority of the eligible Hopi voters did not vote, that it was a minority that voted for the constitution, and that therefore it has never been legal. It is this contention, justifying all their other activities, that has been bought by a number of anthropologists and well-known journalists and national newspapers. Most Hopi are extremely private. They are uncomfortable about being in the public eye, and members of one faction will rarely say anything openly antagonistic about another faction with whom they may disagree. There is, however, the implication that progressives like Alonzo have abandoned the Hopi way. This did not jibe with our impression of Alonzo and his daily striving to fulfill all his traditional obligations. Furthermore, the historical argument of the traditionalists simply does not, it turns out, correspond with the facts.

Ever since the arrival of the white man, there has been considerable internal tension among the Hopi, and the current dispute is only the latest manifestation of this long-simmering discord. It focuses on the legitimacy of the Tribal Council, which was created in 1936. Before then, the Hopi villages were independent. Each had a village leader, called a *kikmongwi*, drawn from the Bear Clan. The kikmongwi was a ritual leader, a "father," for the people of his village. He was responsible for making certain that the many rituals and ceremonial affairs of the village were properly carried out, and he derived his influence from his religious position. He did not deal with politics: other, lesser leaders, acted on his behalf in such matters.

As the U.S. government began, in the twentieth century, to become an ever more constant presence in the Hopi villages (as well as among other Indian tribes), it became apparent that there needed to be a single tribal government

that could deal directly with the federal government. In 1934 Congress passed the Indian Reorganization Act, which codified the government's obligations to protect the rights of Indian tribes and called on the tribes either to adopt a constitutional form of government or to incorporate.

In due course the Hopi decided to adopt a constitution, and one was drafted by the Bureau of Indian Affairs (BIA) in consultation with the village leaders. According to the Act, a majority of the voters had to approve the constitution, and if fewer than 30 percent of the eligible voters voted, the constitution would automatically be rejected. It is on this last point that the traditionalists question the legality of the Tribal Council.

The traditionalists, and their scholarly spokesmen, claim that a 1947 BIA document (*Tribal Relations Pamphlet #1*) shows two figures for the Hopi population: 2,538 in 1935 and 3,444 in 1936. They postulate the larger figure to be the total tribal population and the lower to be the adult population. They go on to challenge the 1937 annual report of Commissioner John Collier of the BIA, which stated that 818 Hopi voted in the referendum (519 for and 299 against), representing about 50 percent of the eligible voting population. Furthermore, they challenge Collier's figures and assert that only 755 people voted, representing only 29 percent of the eligible voters. Thus they argue that the constitution was not ratified.

Yet the 1947 BIA document in question points out, in a conveniently ignored footnote, that the 3,444 figure is actually for the year 1940, not 1936. The tribe had grown in five years. Looking into this matter more closely, in 1979 Wilcomb E. Washburn, a historian of Indian affairs at the Smithsonian Institution, examined another document, the Hopi Tribal Census of 1934, which lists name, sex, age, and other information for a total of 2,605 Hopi, including those living off the reservation in cities. (The numbers showed, with the slight inaccuracy one often finds in these matters, 1,364 adults and 1,257 people under the voting age of twenty-one.) Furthermore, by examining the Navajo Tribal Census for that year, Washburn found an additional 202 Hopi adults and 212 people under twenty-one living in the Moenkopi area in land west of the Hopi mesas.

Thus, even using the lower figure of 755 voters on the constitutional referendum, the total vote represented 48 percent of the eligible voters, not 29 percent, with a total of 33 percent voting yes. By way of comparison, only 34 percent of the U.S. population eligible to vote did so in congressional elections in 1978. In 1981, nearly 80 percent of eligible Hopi voted in the election for Tribal Chairman.

What truly lies at the bottom of the traditionalists' disaffection may never be known. There is a word, *kahopi*, which means "not Hopi." (A member of the tribe who embraces Christianity, for example, is kahopi.) In a sense the Tribal Council can be considered kahopi, since it is a departure from the ancient way in which Hopi have carried on their affairs. But it is there, and most Hopi have adjusted to it and accepted whatever benefits it can bring the people; besides, it has generally sought to act only with the aid of the traditional leaders' wisdom. The question is not whether the Tribal Council should simply disappear; it is how well the Council will, in dealing with the exigencies of twentieth-century America, maintain an environment in which Hopi values and practices—always changing in one way or another—can remain just that: Hopi values and practices.

BELOW: Pickups have become essential for most Hopi families.

RIGHT: Mishongnovi and Shipaulovi seen from the air.

And, it must be said, even the most extreme ideologues often have the germ of reality in their message. The traditionalists—sometimes also called by committed outsiders the Hopi Resistance Movement—are convinced that white culture will bring traditional Hopi values to an end, either by cultural absorption or by bringing about worldwide destruction. They are not alone in this; virtually every Hopi we have met has the same concern, and virtually each one has his or her own way of dealing with it. (Indeed, so individualistic are these people that Page's Law, enunciated only partly in jest, holds that if you find two Hopi agreeing with each other for more than fifteen minutes, one of them is not telling the truth.)

Values do change, however. The mutton used in the ubiquitous Hopi stew was adopted from the Spanish. Some of the Hopi villages now perched on the mesa-tops were down below on the desert until the late 1600s. The pickup has

by and large replaced the burro. And, indeed, since our first visit to Hopi, sedans have become more and more in evidence, bespeaking a growing group of Hopi who work in office jobs and not so much in the fields. As Tribal Chairman Abbott Sekaquaptewa wrote, "Throughout the centuries, Hopi have taken on new things and new ways and adjusted them to Hopi society and made them better. This will continue. We want to supplement Hopi life with the white world's new things and ways, but in our own time and in our own way."

One could argue that living at close quarters in the bustling confines of the villages, with the unavoidable moment-to-moment physical reminders of cultural obligations and lifestyles, is essential to the sustenance of the Hopi way, that moving out of the villages, into places built up in the manner of suburban tracts; with houses far apart, could in the long run lead to the breakdown of the close-knit and, in a sense, urbanized web of relationships and values that have been the basis of Hopi life for a millennium.

But clan relationships have kept Hopi society together for a long time. People in villages fifty miles apart have continued to maintain their mutual relationships and fulfill their obligations. Why should houses placed fifty feet apart make any difference? At this point, no one can say, but many Hopi are opting for the new suburban-style housing—often out of necessity, since that is all that is available to them. Alonzo's family was one.

By 1976, Alonzo's family was deployed as follows. The elder daughter, Jan, lived in Riverside, California, where her husband was employed at the Indian High School. The son, Phillip, with his wife and infant daughter, had just returned to Hopi from cooking school in Chicago. The younger daughter, Dar-

The audience was silent and still; the only sounds were the insistent boom of the drum, heard above the aeolian bass chant of the kachinas and the clacking of turtle shells and the jangle of sleigh bells.

THE **CEREMONIAL YEAR**

JUST WHAT UNLEASHES the human imagination to create a particular culture in a particular geography hangs on an incalculable range of forces including biological inheritance, physical possibility, statistical probability (or chance), and simple obstinate belief. And what kind of culture does arise depends also on whether the sacred and the secular are considered separate and opposite or inseparable gradations of the tissue of reality.

Western civilization, as we are pleased to call it, has evolved a bifurcation of the sacred and the secular. Church on the weekend, business—a different matter—during the week. As Lynn White, a medievalist at the University of California, pointed out in the 1960s, one legacy of the Judeo-Christian tradition is the belief that the earth was created *for* mankind, that mankind could engineer the earth, indeed should alter geography for its own use and however it saw fit. Environmentalists seized upon this

Next to a large kachina doll, Second Mesa's Caralee Secakuku in buckskin leggings gets ready for a ceremony.

historical insight, seeing in it a basic explanation of why we are poisoning our planet at such a rate. They suggested that the new religion of ecology would provide us with the necessary antidote.

At about the same time, environmentalists "discovered" the Indian, and there were many romantic suggestions that Indians were intuitively ecologists, living passively and gently on the land and in harmony with it. Their cultures were perceived as being controlled, as it were, by their geography, not the other way around. But as they sought to join hands with the Indian, environmentalists discovered to their dismay that many Indians lived in rural poverty, with all its unsightly environmental concomitants, and that many Indian tribes seemed content to have their land raped by mineral interests so long as they received proper royalties.

The assumption that the Indians somehow had developed cultures that lived passively on the land, merely taking what it offered them, and only what they needed, was fallacious. The Hopi spend as much time seeking to manage and manipulate the environment as civil engineers do. Their goal is

IN THE PLAZA • The Hopi year, marked by the sun, the planets, and the stars, is a ceremonial year as well, a continuum of sacred and mostly secret rituals conducted in underground chambers called kivas. Most such rituals end in a public ceremony which takes place in the plazas of the villages. There, from January to July, spirit messengers called kachinas dance while the Hopi audience watches and meditates. Most of these ceremonies are for rain.

Other ceremonies, less sacred in nature, are called social dances. On these occasions, unmarried women join male dancers in the plazas to pay respect to various neighboring Indian tribes and commemorate other important features of the Hopi way. Only social dances may be photographed, and only by Hopi. Most Hopi ceremonies are too sacred to be photographed at all.

survival. Their means are not as immediately dramatic or noticeable as building a great dam or a transcontinental highway system, but their techniques have so far proved reliable and enduring.

For a millennium the Hopi have managed their environment by means of their ceremonies: the land and their annual ceremonial cycle are inextricably linked. For an agricultural society in a semi-arid land (technically Hopi is not a desert like the Mojave), it is a matter of survival that the rains be adequate and timely. To see to this, throughout the year the Hopi beseech a pantheon of deities to bless them with moisture in the proper places and at the proper times.

Even the casual visitor notes that Hopi country seems inhospitable, certainly a high-risk area for agriculture. And the facts bear out such first impressions. There are on an average eight to ten inches of precipitation a year, and normally more than half of this falls in the winter months. (By comparison, in northern Virginia eight inches of precipitation in one month is a not-unheard-of figure.) The driest months at Hopi are likely to be May and June, just when the season's first plantings are growing to maturity. One especially dry summer I applauded a July sprinkle and was told a bit dourly by a Hopi farmer that it was too late; he had needed that sprinkle in June. Furthermore, in May there had been too

Scarecrows do not seem to offer much help in the never-ending battle against pests. Ravens, blackbirds, gophers, and plagues of grasshoppers constantly compete with the Hopi for their crops.

heavy a rain; some of his young plants had been washed away and others had rotted. Heavy winds, often experienced in spring, blow sand over the young plants and twist melon vines into hopeless tangles unless an individual windbreak is erected for each plant. The wind also acts as a drying agent, taking away moisture from the ground. And all this is highly erratic. The rain may fall on one field but not on another a few hundred yards away. It is the same with the wind. And beyond the vagaries of the weather, there is also an amplitude of pests. Ravens and crows are uncanny in their timing: they attack the corn just before it is ready to be harvested. They are joined by gophers and rats. And always, throughout the growing season, there is the dry background buzz of grasshoppers.

The Hopi mesas are a place where hardly anyone but the Hopi has ever wanted to be. When the Spanish explorers arrived in the sixteenth century and found no gold or silver to extract, they turned their attention back to the Indian people living in villages (which the Spanish called *pueblos*) along the Rio Grande. Happily, they left the Hopi to a handful of Franciscan padres, who, with little success, sought to extract souls for the Church. Indeed, except for some people from the Rio Grande pueblos who periodically sought refuge at Hopi from the Spanish, and except for raiders from the so-called wild tribes— Ute, Apache, and later Navajo, who roamed the surrounding area in nomadic bands—the Hopi lands were largely avoided by everyone but Hopi until the mid-nineteenth century.

But this is the place where the ancient prophecies had directed the various Hopi clans to gather; it is rare for an Indian tribe to find itself—as the Hopi

do—in the same place now that they occupied before the arrival of the Europeans. Over the centuries they concentrated their settlements on the three southern spurs of the large geological formation called Black Mesa.

Approaching Black Mesa from the east, the traveler sees a high, dark, flat formation rising above the desert floor and stretching across most of the western horizon. It is about 60 miles long and 30 miles wide. It had its essential beginning in the Cretaceous Period, millions of years ago, when much of the region was a shallow inland sea and the world was populated chiefly by reptiles and the creatures spawned in brackish water. (One can see dinosaur tracks at Moenkopi, near Tuba City, and fossilized marine snail shells abound in the dust of the mesas, now nearly 7,000 feet above sea level.)

As sediment from the surrounding lands drained into that unimaginably ancient inland sea, the lower levels of sediment became compressed into porous layers of sandstone. Layer upon layer of sandstone formed, and, for a variety of reasons about which geologists still disagree, the land began to rise; after eons, there was no more inland sea. And all the while the land was rising, wind and water were eroding away the softer rock, leaving the harder, flat mesas and buttes that are the prominent features of the terrain. The important consideration in all this is that underlying the layers of sandstone was a less porous layer of shale, a rock formed by the hardening of clay. As millennium after millennium went by, and the layer cake of the earth's crust thrust itself upward and away from the earth's center and toward the sky, and as the climate changed, Black Mesa was created. Its long-dead plants had here and there been compressed into rich deposits of coal. Its sandstone layers permitted the absorption of rainwater that percolated down until it reached the shale, through which it could not flow. Water, however, is inclined to move, and it moved laterally under Black Mesa, by a variety of routes, collecting in a number of what we call aquifers—underground impoundments of water. And given the slight southward tilt of the land, the water moved to the arid southern spurs of the mesa, where it erupted in what would otherwise appear improbable springs.

About 10,000 years ago, people began to appear on the Colorado Plateau, the vast highland area of the Southwest that includes Black Mesa, and after several thousand years they began to practice agriculture. A thousand years ago the regional climate began to grow drier, and serious local droughts became more frequent. The springs around Black Mesa's southern end must have been an enticement for people seeking a safer place to live. Here there would at least be drinking water. Apparently there has never been enough water from the springs to make any significant irrigation possible, as there was farther south, where people of those earlier times, now called Hohokam, crisscrossed what is now the Phoenix area with a sophisticated spider web of irrigation ditches.

The Hopi clans, following the migration plan spelled out in their prophecies, found pine forests on the northern half of Black Mesa and, to the south, dry scrubland with the occasional piñon pine or juniper and the few springs. There, according to plan, they settled—with a vista extending a hundred miles and with horizons interrupted by unlikely silhouettes of eroded volcanic cones and fortress-like mesas and buttes, a horizon of phantasmagorical outline. They surely recognized that such an environment needed all the intervention they could muster to assure that, despite its waywardness and parsimony, it would also somehow be benign.

•

Along the blacktop highway that winds down the mesa past Shungopavi, there is a crescent of sand among the boulders and slabs of rock that line the shoulder. Susanne and I had pulled off there and walked past the small clutter of rusty cans and broken bottles that such places seem to attract and explored a long, wide ledge overlooking the desert. It was half-past six in the morning, the first morning of our second visit to Hopi, in May 1975. A half hour earlier the sun had

risen over the village of Shipaulovi to the east. Among the dry grass and colorless shrubs were small clusters of Indian paintbrush, sparkling red in the sand. Here and there clumps of white phlox clung to the ground, catching the low, pale sun.

A raven circled noiselessly below us and I listened for sounds but there were none. It was windless and quiet. We stood on one of the flat, circular white rocks that rimmed the ledge and stared at a smaller spur of Second Mesa, which jutted out about half a mile away. Centuries ago, years ago, perhaps just hours ago, yellow slabs had sheared off and tumbled down the slope, joining the giant's rubble strewn below, revealing yet more slabs, more rows of columns inside this great yellow sandstone ruin. I realized that the flat rock we were standing on was the top of another such column and that it too was likely to split off from the cliff at any moment and drop into the canyon below. Everything was still, fixed, but I had a sense of motion—past motion and potential motion—all around me. I would not have been surprised if the column we stood on cracked and crumbled into the canyon. I listened for the sharp crack of rock splitting and heard nothing but silence.

It then occurred to me that I could *hear* the silence. It sounded like the wind blowing ever so lightly somewhere far off—perhaps in the canyon below, perhaps high up on the mesa behind us. But nearby no shrubs, no flowers, no grass stirred. Smoke began to curl up from the rooftops in Shipaulovi.

Employing a technique learned as a boy playing commandos in my backyard, I put my head back, opened my throat and breathed through my mouth so as not to hear my own breathing. I wondered if the elusive sound—the silence I could still hear—was a sound somewhere inside me. It's so quiet here, I thought, you can hear yourself *be*. I wondered if the very silence of this remote place had not promoted the legendary spirituality of the Hopi.

Later that morning, at about ten o'clock, we drove up the road that spirals its way to Shipaulovi to let our friends Linda and Alonzo know we were back in town. We drove slowly, following one pickup truck and followed by another. Above us, a few men scampered down along a footpath from the village proper to a newly built kiva of cinder block. "Something," Susanne said, "is going on here today."

The geography of Shipaulovi is a bit like a wedding cake set on a table, with a road spiraling from layer to layer. On the top layer is the village plaza, with a rock floor overlaid by dusty sand; around it are ranged a number of one-story houses made of stone or (in the case of newer ones) cinder block. On the northern and eastern sides of the plaza, the houses are perched along the edge of the cliff. As you move down from the top layer a few houses and a kiva cling to narrow ledges, connected by the road and precipitous footpaths that wind between stone retaining walls and outhouses. And on the table below, the rest of Shipaulovi's houses are spread out.

On that day, as we inched up the narrow, spiraling dirt road, we noticed that pickups were parked along the various ledges, but we proceeded upward past the last hair-raising switchback to the open space between the houses that define the plaza and those that perch on the western edge of this mesa upon a mesa, the highest point around. A man we recognized but didn't know waved to us. A woman, her head covered with a shawl, emerged through the door of her house carrying a cardboard carton full of fruit. She disappeared past a pile of twisted piñon firewood and over the side of the mesa. We walked between the houses to

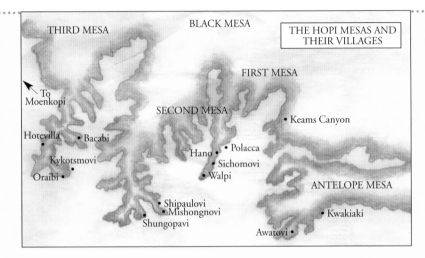

Linda's house on the plaza. There were chairs, mostly inexpensive folding aluminum lawn chairs, arranged around the edge of the plaza, a few of them with old Hopi ladies in shawls sitting in them. Two boys, about six years old, chased each other across the dusty plaza. A few people were standing on the roofs of the houses. Apparently a ceremony was about to take place.

"Come in, come in,nswer to our knock. The small room was crowded with people. "Oh, it's you. It's *you!*" Linda cried. Her daughter Darlene grabbed Susanne's hand. "Susanne, Susanne," the girl said, repeating her name in a kind of chant.

"Sit down, sit down," Linda urged, and we found places. We learned that a dance was indeed about to take place in the plaza, a dance in behalf of the recently planted corn, and that soon the kachinas would be coming. They had been there the day before (that is, Saturday) and would return any minute now.

Hopiland is surrounded by Navajo neighbors, and the dance both honors and makes fun of them.

Perched on small chairs placed against the walls of the room were a number of women, some corralling small children who were twisting and turning in the women's clutches, from time to time extricating themselves explosively and leaping across the room like so many pinballs. On the whitewashed walls hung foot-high kachina dolls, small models of the Hopi spirit messengers who come to the plaza to dance. The dolls were gifts from the kachinas to deserving girl children, not only as a kind of generous blessing but as a means of teaching the children to distinguish—by familiarity—among the many kinds of kachinas who watch over them and their parents and other relatives.

There were no introductions, and everyone spoke Hopi when the conversation resumed. We sat quietly, feeling welcome and accepted. A number of the women looked a lot like Linda; they were, we learned later, her blood sisters.

After about a half hour of the breathy lilt of Hopi conversation had bounced bewilderingly by us, the women began to stand up and, pulling their shawls about them, moved to the door that opened from the dark room into the plaza. We followed and took seats on a cinder-block retaining wall in the cool shadow. The plaza had filled with people, mostly women sitting in rows three or four deep around the edges of the plaza, wearing multicolored shawls that were predominantly either maroon or navy blue. Children rushed back and forth, in the dust, some of them competing for possession of an elusive ball. Dogs scuttled around the corners of the buildings. On the roofs around the plaza people had assembled in rows, mostly younger people, teenagers of both sexes. The hubbub of the expectant audience died down when, through the southern end of the plaza, a long line of identically dressed dancers—the kachinas—emerged

between two houses. There were about thirty of them. Their heads were white and black and turquoise, and they had cylindrical red beaks with yellow tips. Each had a mane of spruce boughs, and spruce shoots stuck out from various parts of their clothing. They wore white skirts shaped like kilts and long sashes around their waists. In back, foxtails hung down from the sashes, and these and the white fringes of the sashes swayed as they walked into the plaza, forming a long line. Each held a sprig of spruce in the left hand and a gourd rattle in the right. And tied on their calves were sleigh bells and turtle-shell rattles that jingled and clattered with each step. A drummer, holding a large round drum covered with deerskin, and a white-haired man in a shirt and trousers, with a red bandanna tied around his head, accompanied them into the plaza.

Abruptly, and in synchrony with the drum, the kachinas began a low, mournful, and rhythmic chant, a deep bass, and they began to dance, stamping their moccasined feet on the ground and moving their hands alternately up and down, the rattles' sound adding to the slight offbeat of the turtle shells and sleigh bells. The sun beat down as the long line of kachinas chanted and moved slowly, first in one direction, then in the other, an occasional hesitation step interrupting their steady stomping. The white-haired man moved up and down the line, sprinkling the kachinas with cornmeal as if, by that gesture, he were feeding them, and he called out occasional instructions. The audience was silent and still; the only sounds were the insistent boom of the drum, heard above the aeolian bass chant of the kachinas and the clacking of turtle shells and the jangle of sleigh bells. After several minutes, the drum stopped, as did the chant, with a descending *oooooaaaw* and the hiss of a single rattle. There was a fragment of

Linda Quavehema collects the extremely sharp-ended yucca shoots from the desert. She will dry them for use in making plaques for ceremonial and gift-giving uses.

silence and suddenly the line of dancers began another chant: the plaza was filled with their single voice, the people riveted by their pounding rhythm and the thunder of the drum. Though I knew I was among the tallest people in the plaza, the kachinas seemed huge to me as I sat among the Hopi women on the low cinder-block wall.

After twenty long minutes, the chanting kachinas filed out, leaving the drum behind in the plaza. As if out of nowhere, six bizarre individuals, wearing cut-off shorts and sneakers, their bodies painted with what seemed to be yellow clay, appeared in the plaza, shouting and racing up and down, back and forth. These were, we assumed, the clowns who, we had heard, appear in some kachina dances. Children laughed. A number of women covered their heads with their shawls and disappeared into the houses, to re-emerge carrying food in bags and cartons which they put in the center of the plaza. The clowns received the food gratefully and boisterously, shouting, *Kwa-kwai!* (I later discovered that this was the male word for "thank you.") Crudely lettered in black on their backs were the names of television characters—Chico, Flip, Sanford-N-Son—and one was labeled Fat Albert, another Pres. Ford. They carried on raucously, commandeering the drum and caricaturing the dance of the kachinas, calling loudly to the people on the rooftops, swallowing soda pop and regurgitating it, taking turns photographing each other with a Polaroid camera that had mysteriously appeared, all the while shouting, "No pictures! No pictures!"

After a few minutes a group of pink-faced figures arrived, each carrying a sack on the end of a stick like a hobo. The clowns took exaggerated note of these newly arrived ragamuffins, loudly designated them as "Mr. Cambodia,"

"Mr. Vietnam," "Mr. Puerto Rico," and so forth, and ordered them to sit down and eat. As they sat there, the clowns loudly introduced them to various "mothers" in the audience and at the same time tweaked and pushed them. "It's Mother's Day today," one of the clowns explained (in fact it was), and once the introductions were over, the clowns marched the pink-faced hoboes off like so many refugees.

Next a band of dancers wearing black kilts and with pinkish-brown bodies and heads arrived. Each head had three brown knobs—one on each side and one on top—and a comical little brown beak like a bird's. These mudheads (as we later learned they were called) began to dance to their own muffled low chanting. The clowns took note of this for a few minutes and then leaped on them, knocking them to the ground. A melee ensued: several old women left their seats and joined the fray, helping the clowns to smack the mudheads on their bottoms and pulling their kilts up and their shorts down, much to the amusement of the audience.

As abruptly as the fight had started, it ended. The women bustled back to their seats and the clowns and mudheads joined in tossing into the audience candy, fruit, and bread, as well as cans of soft drinks, from the clowns' cartons in the middle of the plaza. The mudheads then left the plaza and the clowns withdrew to the sidelines, as the kachinas began to reappear. As the full complement of kachinas assembled, forming a semicircle, the atmosphere changed from the boisterous, slapstick mood of the clowns' interlude back to a somber and to us almost ominous mood as the kachinas began their awesome chanting and broke, as one, into the repetitive stomping in alternate directions.

Dough made from store-bought flour and formed into spherical loaves is set out on a kitchen table before baking. Less than an hour later, the baker removes the fragrant fresh loaves from her oven perched on the edge of the mesa.

In my notebook I hurriedly scribbled down the names the clowns had on their backs; they were getting smeared during their antics. An old woman behind me said, "No." Another said, "He's drawing." I said I was only writing down some names, and put the notebook away. The white-haired man with the red bandanna immediately left the dancing semicircle of kachinas and headed in my direction. Standing over me, he asked to see what I was doing. I showed him the notebook, and he took it and returned with it to the kachinas. I was still in the shade of the house behind me, and though it was cool I began to sweat and wished I could become invisible. After one circuit of the line of kachinas, during which the old man dusted them with cornmeal, he came back to where I was sitting, held out my notebook to me in what seemed a preternaturally large brown hand with a long, horny thumbnail, and forcefully cautioned me to write no more.

The kachinas alternated with the clowns several times, and then, after noon, they entered the plaza in ones and twos, carrying sacks of freshly baked Hopi bread, which they placed in the center of the plaza; then they formed a line and began to dance.

After another twenty minutes, the kachinas approached the sacks of bread in the center of the plaza and began hurling loaves into the audience, peering like great birds down into the sacks and lobbing bread to the women in the chairs, pegging it vigorously to the people on the roofs.

And so it went through the rest of the afternoon—the solemn kachinas alternating with the raucous clowns, the entire proceedings punctuated by the athletic distribution of food and occasionally, to children, of kachina dolls and miniature bows and arrows. The whole time I had the panicky feeling that the

clowns, being unpredictable rowdies, might at any moment single me out for my transgression with the notebook and haul me into the plaza to inflict some further humiliation. For during the afternoon they grew rowdier, pulling individuals out of the crowd and forcing them to participate in their increasingly boisterous and bawdy carryings-on. Toward the end of the afternoon the clowns were, indeed, actively taunting the kachinas as they danced. But soon other kachinas, some in the form of animals and birds, arrived, and eventually the kachinas whipped the clowns into submission with sheaves of yucca. It was painful to watch.

At the end of the last dance, like the climax in a display of fireworks, a truly prodigious amount of stuff was hurled by the kachinas into the audience: cans, loaves of bread, candy, gum, cigarettes, all filled the air for as much as fifteen minutes. A man standing near me simultaneously caught a can of pop in his right hand and a banana between his left elbow and his side. Then the kachinas filed out of the plaza and the people picked up their folding chairs and drifted away. Susanne and I stayed for a while as the plaza emptied, watching small bands of children chase each other among the cardboard cartons and litter, all that was left of the food that had been prepared by the Hopi women or bought from the supermarket. We noticed that the sky had grown cloudy, and we drove off in wonderment at the extraordinary lavishness of the ceremony.

Ceremonially the Hopi year is a continuum, but the kachinas visit the villages during only about half of the year. Toward the end of July they return to their spiritual home in the San Francisco Peaks, the great volcanic cone just north of Flagstaff with the highest mountain in Arizona (rising 12,636 feet above sea level) on its rim. It is a group of peaks cloaked in evergreen trees and surmounted by boulders of naked lava scree. Visible from most of the villages though almost a hundred miles of the Painted Desert lie between, the Peaks, a constant presence, is a source of clouds that, if the Hopi have done well, will build up over the cinder-colored top and tear themselves away, moving northeast toward the Hopi mesas to spill their life-giving rain on the sandy patches of ground where the Hopi grow corn.

San Francisco Peaks, where the kachinas live half the year, is where these spirits rehearse, as one Hopi friend put it, the quintessential performance, the making

of rain, that makes virtually everything else possible. The word kachina (or, more purely rendered, *katsina*) means "respected spirit." The kachinas are supernaturals, the spirits of all things in the universe, of rocks, stars, animals, plants, and ancestors who have lived good lives. As the spirits of nature, they are believed to have a certain amount of control over nature, including the weather. They can take up human-like form, as when they appear in the villages, and they are the guardians of Hopi life. They act as messengers to gods such as the sun, as well as to the ultimate god, or spirit, that created everything and is implicit in everything.

So for six months the kachinas do not appear physically in the villages. These towering, determined, awesome figures are not visible, are not there performing their powerful ceremonies, chanting their hymns, providing with unimaginable generosity, not to mention an amusing athleticism, offerings of food and magical gifts for the children.

Consider all this from the viewpoint of a Hopi child, for whom the autumn stretches out almost endlessly—with all its activity—into colder days, shorter days, early dark as the sun sets farther north. You eat the first and the last meal of the day in a stove-heated kitchen. Outside it is dark: it is drawing near to the pahanas' Christmas and to what you have learned is the shortest day of the year, the winter solstice, when the sun appears only briefly in its arc over the mesas. It is about to reach its winter house. You have tried to be good, to do your parents' bidding, your teacher's bidding, and you have tried to remember what the kachinas would consider right, and of course you know that you have failed to one degree or another. You picked on your sister, you deserted the woodpile and its urgent requirements for a quick game of basketball. You even sassed your

At Shipaulovi, a woman removes bread from her oven. Next to the oven is a fiery hole where a pudding is cooking. In the background, a kiva is perched on the edge of the mesa.

Like children everywhere, Hopi children enjoy sucking on an icicle, giggling, and cuddling dolls. Hopi ceremonies are directed at all mankind, but they clearly focus on the most beloved element of their population—their children.

mother once and, your uncles being in another village and not hearing immediately of the event, you got away with it. It's cold outside, and inside you feel a little lonely. Meanwhile you notice a heightening of activity in your home. Your mother mentions to your father that her hands are sore from making piki. She spends a lot of time making round loaves of Hopi bread in her outdoor oven. Your father spends more time after supper out of the house; he goes to the kiva to "make preparations." Something important is about to happen; a great turning, an arrival is imminent.

Then, one afternoon, a lone figure appears to the south and makes its way uncertainly into the village. It is the Soyal kachina, wearing an old and tattered deerskin hunting shirt and carrying four long switches with feathers attached to them. Its head is red and turquoise. It sings to itself in so muted a voice that no one can make out the words, and it totters around the village as if feebly emerging from a dormant state. It pauses to perform a dance, haltingly, like an old man, visiting the kivas and the plaza. As quietly as it came, it goes. It is now all right for the other kachinas to visit the village.

In ensuing days, other kachinas arrive and perform many crucial functions, all having to do with reawakening the sleeping, almost dead, world of winter. The sun must have help to turn back toward its summer house. The kivas must be opened up for the kachinas. Seed corn of all colors must be consecrated in the kiva and shown by corn maidens to the village before being returned to the kiva. Prayer feathers (*pahos*) must be made—for family and friends, for houses, beasts of burden (now including passenger vehicles), domestic animals, fields, and crops—and distributed.

To some of these prayer feathers the men transfer all the badness and evil that have accumulated in their bodies and spirits during the year. These feathers are then taken out and hung on bushes at certain shrines until the winter winds blow them away, taking with them the poisons of the previous year. This is to prevent anyone's coming in contact with them and being infected. The precaution appears to be more than merely symbolic.

A pahana woman, we were told, was staying at the Hopi Cultural Center motel at this time of year and became extremely ill in the middle of the night. In agony, she was taken to the Public Health Service hospital some twenty miles east, at Keams Canyon, where the doctors found nothing wrong with her. She returned to the motel the next morning, where the manager explained diffidently that the cleaning woman had found in the visitor's room that morning a small cache of pahos that she had picked up from here and there, wherever the wind had blown them, feathers bearing spiritual bile built up by Hopi during the year. Realizing her error, the visitor returned these tainted messengers to the desert where she had found them, canceled the remainder of her reservation at the motel, and left, relieved and well.

With the Soyal ceremony, the new year begins, and the season of the kachinas is under way. There are some 300 different kachinas, certain ones appearing in certain villages and not in others. From an early age Hopi children learn to distinguish them—to learn the roles they play in Hopi life and the varied symbolism embodied in their colors and other elements of their appearance. Kachinas represent many of the things that are important in the Hopi world—animals such as antelopes, owls, or eagles, historical figures who played a crucial role in

Once in the plaza the Buffalo dancers will perform for about twenty minutes, accompanied by a group of men who sing songs to the rhythm of a single drummer. When they are finished, the singers and dancers leave the plaza and another group enters. Alternating, the two groups keep the plaza filled with sound, color, and movement from morning till dusk for two full days.

ancient events, plants both domestic and wild, even mountains. Individually and in the aggregate, they are largely benevolent figures, intermediaries between the Hopi and the "rain people" and other supernatural spirits.

As Emory Sekaquaptewa, a member of the Eagle Clan from Hotevilla, now a linguist at the University of Arizona, wrote, recalling his own childhood perspective: "The kachina is all goodness and all kindness. The kachina also gives gifts to children in all its appearances. Thus it is rather difficult for me to agree with the descriptions of the kachina that often appear in literature. The kachina is frequently described as being grotesque, but the Hopi child does not perceive the kachina as grotesque. By his conduct toward the child, the kachina demands good behavior."

It is, the child soon learns, a reciprocal arrangement. The kachinas have the power to arrange for rain, which is what the Hopi deeply desire. But the Hopi have certain things that the kachinas want: pahos and cornmeal, for example. The kachinas enjoy dancing in the Hopi plazas. And they like to see goodness and sincerity on the part of the Hopi. So it is not surprising that in many of the kachina ceremonies mutual gift-giving is an all-important element.

In January there is usually a Buffalo Dance in one or two villages; this is called a "social" dance because both men and unmarried women from the villages participate, dancing in pairs of couples. The unmarried women, often young girls, wear a black eye-covering, which of course obscures their vision, and they keep their faces expressionless. We were told that the men dancers, who range in age from the twenties up to the sixties, try to make their partners laugh by performing particularly tricky steps. This testing is part of the discipline, the training involved in growing up.

Though not specifically religious, the social dances require a great deal of preparation in the kiva, rehearsing the songs and the steps, and purifying oneself by fasting and ritual washing of the hair. And after the end of the Buffalo Dance, always a two-day affair, the buffalos run out of town and are symbolically shot by the villagers (the rifle fire is alarmingly real), thus permitting the buffalo spirits to go forth and report to their kind and the spirit people that the Hopi have faithfully discharged their duties and lived up to the high standard expected of them. The Buffalo Dance commemorates the old days when the Hopi made use of the wide-ranging herds of buffalo, or bison, and it is also a prayer for moisture.

Buffalo Dances, like other social dances, are not as deeply religious as the plaza dances of the kachinas, and thus they can be photographed—by Hopi, There was a time, around the turn of the century and earlier, when the Hopi did not seem to mind photography of even their sacred ceremonies. A number of missionaries would march into the midst of kiva ceremonies and remove objects from altars to photograph them outside in the light; there are photographs now routinely published of actual society altars—items that should not be seen even by a Hopi who is not of the particular society, or priesthood. Finding their most sacred and intimate objects on public view, the Hopi decided around 1910 to forbid photographs and sketches (now also tape recordings) of their sacred ceremonies. They remain to this day open to the public in certain instances, such as the plaza dances at some villages, but most aspects of the Hopi ceremonies are now, altogether appropriately, reserved for Hopi eyes and ears.

On a certain day in February, the kachinas bring bean sprouts into the villages—bean sprouts that have somehow grown in the dead of winter. They give them, along with traditional gifts—rattles, dolls, and sticks carved and painted to represent lightning—to the children of the village, signaling that the growing season is soon to begin. Later that day, adults prepare the bean sprouts in a special soup, while the children play with their gifts from the kachinas.

In February a miracle occurs. The land is generally locked in the last and deepest throes of winter, with freezing winds and, in a good year, snow. Nothing seems alive on the plains below. Those who do not work at regular jobs huddle around wood and coal stoves inside their houses. Then, of a morning, a figure comes forth from a shrine—Crow Mother in a white robe with the black wings of the crow rising up beside her head. Crow Mother sings a frail, quiet song recounting the history of the kachinas; she carries a basket full of foot-long, freshly grown, tender bean sprouts. These are the miracle: bean sprouts that have somehow grown in the short, dark days of winter, testimony to the power of the kachina called Muyingwa, the principal deity of germination.

Later in the day, a kaleidoscopic host of other kachinas emerge from the kivas, and they promenade throughout the village during the day, handing out to the women and children bean sprouts and then toys and gifts—bows and arrows, rattles, and dolls. Warrior and other frightening kachinas with bulging eyes patrol the village, taunting some of the other kachinas and providing discipline in the event of any untoward activity—such as getting in the way of the promenading kachinas—on the part of the audience.

The Bean Dance is a renewal, an invocation to the kachinas to intercede in behalf of the seeds that will soon be planted. The Hopi plant more than twenty varieties of beans, along with corn and other vegetables and fruits. The longer the bean sprouts that the kachinas bring from the kiva, the better will be the growing season. The Bean Dance is a reminder also for the children of the largess of the kachinas.

Bean Dance time is also when ten- and eleven-year-olds are initiated into the kachina society, the first of a long series of steps into spiritual adulthood. In the late afternoon the initiates are led by a godparent (chosen by the child and its parents the previous summer) into the kiva, where they are told the story of the kachinas. At one point, according to a Third Mesa account, Crow Mother and some whipper kachinas arrive on the scene suddenly and alarmingly. The godparents lead the initiates to the whippers, who, encouraged by Crow Mother's recitation of their youthful sins, whip the initiates, giving each one four blows with fresh yucca shoots, raising welts, even breaking the skin. (Earlier, Crow Mother and the whippers have trooped through the village whipping others—adults—who presented themselves for this cleansing ordeal.)

Later that night, about eleven o'clock, people begin to line up outside the kiva and eventually are admitted by a man serving as the father of the kachinas. The women go through the side door and (as at a dance we attended in Kykotsmovi) sit in rows in the south end of the kiva, which is raised slightly above the main area. Men visitors descend the ladder from the roof, to be greeted by the women, who call out, asking the men to enter carefully and urging them to make themselves at home. The men move to the right of the ladder and sit on banquettes along the north and east walls. On the west side sit several young maidens, and to the right of the ladder, on the eastern side, sit the young initiates, wrapped in blankets.

Presently one hears a rattle up on the roof. The father of the kachinas, sitting at the base of the ladder, calls out for the kachinas to enter, joined in this invitation by the women. A drummer descends—either a clown or a mudhead or

some other—followed by the kachinas, who make sounds, such as growls, peculiar to their kind, and file around, handing out gifts to the initiates, to form a circle open to the south. The father of the kachinas, welcoming them, moves along the line, "feeding" them with cornmeal; as he reaches the middle of the line a kachina rattles his gourd, the drummer begins in earnest, and the kachinas begin their chant, swaying and dancing. Looming above the visitors, all at close quarters, they fill the kiva with sound, and the drumbeat reverberates from the walls and the ceiling, becoming palpable in one's very bloodstream.

After about fifteen minutes the kachinas file out, bestowing gifts of food on the initiates, the maidens, and, in some cases, the visitors. Soon there is the sound of another rattle on the roof, and another group of kachinas is invited in. At the dance we attended, there were three groups of kachinas (one for each kiva in the village), and after all three groups had danced, each group of kachinas returned again, and danced two dances. By about half-past three in the morning the ceremony was over, and the visitors filed out, going around the other side of the ladder, the south side, in order to complete the circle, leaving the kachinas and the initiates and their godparents behind.

The kachinas bring both blessings and warnings. Some of the songs are prayers for what the Hopi want—rain, good crops, a good and long life—and some are admonitions, pointing out what the Hopi have done wrong and what they must do to mend their ways. The kachinas dance to help the Hopi to meditate, to pray silently. We were unaware of the specific words or content of the songs we heard that night, but as we left the kiva and walked through the dark, silent village, lit only here and there by a streetlight or light from the windows

of Hopi returning home, we felt drained and at the same time exhilarated, almost overcome by the pulse of the music still reverberating inside us, and yet pervaded by a sense of total well-being.

Back in the kiva, the young initiates would complete their entry into the kachina society; at dawn they would be taken home to have their hair ritually washed and to receive a new name, signaling this important rite of passage.

Most, though not all, Hopi are initiated into the kachina society. There are later initiations as well—into the men's and women's societies. Again, not everyone initiated into the kachina society goes further. And beyond the men's societies, there are yet other priesthoods—the One Horn society, the Two Horn society, and the Singers. Many men, by choice, do not enter these priesthoods—nor, in fact, is every man allowed to enter them. These priesthoods carry with them awesome and for the most part secret responsibilities for the religious affairs of the Hopi people. Membership in these societies is not based on clan. Each society has special knowledge and special wisdom, unknown even to the other societies. We have been told that the One Horn society has the responsibility of giving a newly appointed Bear Clan leader (or kikmongwi) the authority to carry out the duties of his office. The One Horns, we were told, are enforcers, often with rather grim duties, such as eliminating intruders into the initiation rites of the men's societies. The Two Horns are philosophers, and the Singers consecrate decisions that are made. It is in these societies that the truly deep Hopi religion lies, where the true meaning of the Hopi past is interpreted, where the true knowledge lies of the beginning, the meaning, and the end of life. This is

the part of Hopi religion that is completely secret and cannot properly be discussed with outsiders.

Throughout the ensuing weeks other so-called kiva dances, known as Following Dances, will take place, merging finally into dances in the plazas as the weather changes. But in the meantime the other, complementary role that the kachinas play—the disciplinary—is seen at its-most vivid. The ogres are coming—the *soyokos*. One day Soyoko Wuhti, the ogre woman, arrives in the village to warn that the ogres will soon arrive in force. Several days later, a remarkable procession takes place, much to the anxiety of Hopi children, who listen fearfully as the lugubrious chants and terrifying hoots draw ever closer. Inevitably the awful sounds are heard right outside the door, and the child's name is called. The mother (or an uncle) takes the child reluctantly to the door, to be confronted by a huge and hideous woman, red tongue hanging out between perilous fangs. She has a basket strapped to her back for taking away children. It is Soyoko. She is attended by a frightful band of other ogres, many wearing crazily awkward feather headdresses and armed with knives and axes and saws, their long red-and-black beaks clacking rows of sharp white teeth together.

In a loud voice so that all can hear, the mother explains that the child has been good. Soyoko disagrees and reaches out, saying that she knows the child sassed its mother and doesn't bathe enough. Well, perhaps, the mother says, but she knows the child will be good from now on. The frightening ogre, who seems to know everything, disagrees: the child is to be punished for those transgressions and for not doing its homework. Soyoko will put the child in her basket and take it away and eat it.

The mother remonstrates. She offers Soyoko some meat in the child's stead and she promises to see that the homework will be done properly. An aunt produces a rat, and Soyoko roars with disapproval and grabs the child's arm, hauling it into the plaza. All right, all right, the mother pleads, here is a rabbit. The soyoko grumbles, looks at the rabbit, and eventually places it in her basket. The child is off the hook.

Not quite. One of the terrible beaked ogres approaches with a saucepan and hands it to Soyoko, who then, in front of everyone ranged about the plaza, peering out of their doors at the child's humiliation, pours water over its head in the ancient and mortifying ritual of Hopi purification.

On the occasions when we have been present at the arrival of this absolutely terrifying band, we have kept well to the rear, in the shadows of the house, hoping not to hear our own names called. One little girl of our acquaintance was admonished not to speak "so much pahana," and a small boy, aged two, was forced to march tearfully to the precipitous edge of the mesa and throw his baby bottle over the side. He was too old, the soyoko judged, for such infantile satisfactions. Once we saw Soyoko complain to a woman in her twenties that she played too much basketball, to the detriment of her household chores; she was hauled into the plaza and required to demonstrate her basketball skills while the ogres carried on a humiliating commentary about her lack of talent. And things can get quite rough. One young girl we know was hauled kicking and screaming into the plaza, clutching her grandmother. Outraged by the resistance, Soyoko pulled harder, and the grandmother was jerked to the ground, spraining her wrist.

Child psychiatrists may pale at such autocratic punishment, so harsh an instilling of discipline and social values—but we have heard a number of elementary schoolteachers wish they had so useful an ally. Frightening as it is, there is a highly positive side to this tradition. Rarely, one Hopi confided to us, do the children get taken away by Soyoko and eaten. Instead, they are ultimately spared, thanks to the intercession of their parents and aunts and uncles. Emory Sekaquaptewa described the details of an elaborate example of this side of the Soyoko experience:

A boy, "barely six years old, had misbehaved and was threatened with the appearance of the Soyoko, who would come and take him away because he had misbehaved. So on the day of the arrival of the kachinas, the parents had planned that when the kachinas came to the door, they would send the child outside, and the mother would appear with the child and inform the kachinas in all seriousness that it was not right and timely for them to come after him, because he was going to be married. He was a groom, and until this very important ceremony was completed he was not available. So the kachinas demanded some proof. They were very persistent, so after much drama and emotion the bride was brought out to show there really was a marriage ceremony going on. The bride turned out to be the old grandmother, who was dressed in the full paraphernalia of a bride. Then bride and groom appealed as a pair to the kachinas that this was indeed an important ceremony. Obviously when there is a marriage, the relations on both sides are very interested in the preservation of the union. So the relatives all intervened, and soon they outnumbered the kachinas, and thus the child was saved. The child not only learned the importance of good behavior, but this drama also strengthened his security by showing him that there are people who do come to his aid."

LEFT: Navajo dancers file into the plaza.

BELOW RIGHT: In beads, feathers, and shades, Darlene Quavehema portrays a cool young Navajo woman for a day.

From late March into July, in one village or another, and often in more than one, the kachinas come to the plaza on most weekends. These ceremonies, like most other Hopi ceremonies, are timed to precede and thereby benefit the various plantings of crops. Traditionally, the chief of the Sun Clan of each village would keep track of the important dates by seeing when the sun rose over or set behind one or another point of reference on the distant horizon. The sun is still carefully observed, but given the changing nature of employment on the reservation, the precise timing of the sun must be somewhat adjusted so that the ceremonies can take place on the weekends.

The activity of the clowns at these plaza dances commands the audience's attention but has not received the attention it merits from chroniclers of Hopi. The clowns are of course on hand to entertain the audience in the temporary absence of the kachinas—but that is not their chief function. In a society in which virtually everything has at least one level of symbolic meaning, the clowns must certainly be more than entertainment. In each appearance they are, during the course of a two-day-long kachina ceremony, repeating the Hopi version of *Everyman,* in a morality play that is always the same. Despite the spontaneous appearance of their shenanigans, the clowns proceed through a fairly set series of steps, or levels, until the ultimate and inevitable denouement.

The clowns arrive from the rooftops, the opposite direction from that of the original Hopi, who came here from a world below. They proceed immediately to lose grace. Admiring the kachinas, they pridefully seek to emulate them, creating a crude and slapstick caricature of the kachinas' stately dance.

They are gluttonous and lascivious: they seek to amass great quantities of material goods and they pinch girls. They also emulate the ways of the pahana, talking English and riding motorcycles. As their fall from grace becomes more and more pronounced, they begin actively taunting the kachinas. Then, toward the end of the second day, appears a lone figure, the owl kachina, who tries to warn the clowns, waving a yucca switch at them. (Hopi consider the owl the announcer of the end, the prophet of doom. It is extremely unfortunate to have an owl appear nearby, for it presages the end of someone's life. A friend once found an owl sitting on the hood of his pickup truck. He tried to shoot it, but it got away. Later that day he discovered that his grandfather had died just about the time the owl had lighted on his truck.)

The clowns, of course, ignore the warning of the owl kachina, and soon a number of other kachinas run menacingly into the plaza—these are whippers. While the other kachinas continue their ceremonial dance, taking no notice of the melee around them, the whippers, directed by the owl kachina, proceed to chase down the clowns, who are still unaware of the trouble they face. Finally the chief clown realizes what is happening and tries to make a deal with the owl to commute the punishment of death to a sound thrashing. The owl agrees, and the clowns are caught and severely whipped, their possessions seized, their clothes ripped. They are doused in water and sometimes threatened with snakes. Finally, beaten and subdued, they agree to follow the true path.

With wonderfully comic variations on the theme, the clowns, each time they appear, play out this morality tale—yet another reminder to all present, even Hopi priests, that it is easy to lose the true way, and perhaps the classic

demonstration that the Hopi sense of humor is an essential part of even their most sacred wisdom. Good and evil, the sacred and the profane, are, in this healthy world view, all part of human nature, distinguishable ends of a spectrum with many gradations in between.

In late July the kachinas make their last appearance of the year, in the Niman ceremony. This is the Home Dance (*niman* means "to go home"); after it is over, the kachinas leave the villages and return to San Francisco Peaks, bearing with them their observations of how well the Hopi have been carrying out their duties and their prayers for a better life. This time of the year seems to be pervaded by a special kind of reverence, a special awesomeness. The last crops have been planted and the first crop of corn has been harvested. It is a crucial time in the growing season and, of course, a kind of climax in the kachina cycle. The Home Dance is of special importance to the brides of the previous year, and it also directly involves some other Hopi messengers, who for a month or so have been sitting patiently on the roofs of the village, observing through the sharpest eyes known in nature the day-to-day efforts of the Hopi to lead lives of excellence. These are eagles.

During the day the kachinas dance, and several female kachinas (*manas*) symbolically grind corn before them. Toward the end of the day various society priests and matriarchs emerge from the kivas and bless the kachinas, sprinkling them with water from medicine bowls and with cornmeal, blowing smoke from clay pipes on them, and giving them pahos, transferring the prayers to the Niman kachinas to take home. The pahos are considered, among other things, as "raiment" for these spirits.

Then, after the last song, the father of the kachinas speaks. He acknowledges that the kachinas are ready to go back to the rain people. After the day-long

dance, he says, the kachinas are tired. He asks them not to tarry when they have reached their home but to return soon with rain so that the harvest will be good and the Hopi will be able to feed their children. The Hopi are happy and certain that the rain people await the kachinas and will rejoice to see them.

The next day, at dawn, a white-clad kachina called Eototo, the chief of all the kachinas, climbs out of a kiva, accompanied by four other kachinas, who take up positions at the four corners of the kiva roof. In the thin light of daybreak a lengthy ritual is performed in silence. Then the kachinas return underground into the kiva, and the kachina season is over. Thus do the kachinas of Hopi go home, in late July, to the source of moisture, to the trees and medicinal herbs—the life-giving altitudes of San Francisco Peaks.

Almost immediately, preparations must begin for the next phase of the ceremonial year, the ceremonies that take place in August. These are the Snake Dance and the Flute Dance.

The Snake Dance holds a special fascination for the outside world, and for Hopi as well. A lot of people have a fear of snakes. It is no wonder that this ceremony, in the course of which men hold snakes, including rattlers some four feet long, in their mouths, draws throngs. It is a relatively short public ceremony, preceded by eight days of secret ritual preparation.

For four days the snake priests have walked off in the four directions into the plains below the mesas looking for snakes, collecting them and bringing them back to the kiva. On a fifth day, they go in all directions, no doubt to make sure the snake complement is adequate. Anthropologists, herpetologists, and other experts have sought to discover what the Hopi snake priests do with the snakes in the kiva

to render them so unresistant to the manipulations that will soon occur publicly. Some suggest that they feed the snakes to make them lethargic, which they patently are not. Some suggest that they milk them of venom, which the Hopi snake priests deny. They have no need, they say, to do this to their "little brothers." No one really knows what happens between the snakes and the snake priests. After contemplating this mystery, along with a number of others that occur on the mesas, I concluded that what happened between the snakes and the snake priests was no more my business than it was that of the Hopi not ritually involved.

One August day in 1975, as I sat with Alonzo on his back stoop high above the desert, he said, "There's one of the snake priests coming back." I saw nothing but the rolling brown land between Shipaulovi and First Mesa, dotted here and there with the more or less geometrical outlines of Hopi fields. "Where?" I asked. "Along the trail," Alonzo said. I suggested using the binoculars that I had inside, and he agreed.

Alonzo observed the priest through the binoculars for only a moment when another Hopi, some twenty feet away, began to yell. Alonzo slipped me the binoculars—apparently too much a pahana intrusion—and I hastened inside and put them away. Eventually, in the gathering afternoon shadow, I saw the snake priest in question making his way along the lumpy foothills of the mesa below, carrying a sack. Full of snakes.

"We used to do the Snake Dance here in Shipaulovi; it was my clan's responsibility. But the Bear Clan here decided that they would do it, so they took it away from us. They didn't do nothing with it. Then after a while they asked us if we would take it back. Our uncles had told us this would happen, that it

one can—as we have found—gain an enriching feeling of peace and accomplishment through making such a commitment of time and attention.

In August, after the Snake Dance, the Hopi Cultural Center motel empties of tourists and well-wishers, but the ceremonial season continues. The women's dances, of which there are three types, now take place. One of these is the Basket Dance, which we saw performed in Shipaulovi. Periodically throughout the day, groups of women entered the plaza, forming a circle. They were dressed in *mantas,* the traditional black dresses of Hopi, embroidered with bright red and bright green, and carried yucca plaques. Once the circle was formed, the women began a slow, nasal, and somehow wistful song, their eyes cast down. The song is in behalf of the fertility of the land and of the Hopi. In the midst of the circle, led there by a male priest who made a path for them with a trail of cornmeal, were three other women, without plaques.

As the circle of women began their song, the three in the center began to hurl food and baskets and bread and spatulas and boxes of animal crackers and heaven knows what into the assembled onlookers. With each strong-armed delivery there was a shout from the crowd, and the men and boys leaped, like basketball players intent on a rebound, for these gifts. In mid-afternoon it rained and the plaza got muddy and slippery; the men jumped and sloshed about in the mud, wrestling over the largess. The rest of the people hooted with laughter and appreciation. Unmindful of the chaos of generosity that was going on throughout the day, the circle of women moved their plaques in rhythm with their prayers. At the end, all the women gathered near a kiva outside the plaza and threw food and other appreciated objects into the surrounding crowd.

Midway through the Basket Dance, just before it began to rain, Hopi men began to appear, running into the plaza in sneakers and shorts; these were the finishers in a race that had started miles away below the mesa and was associated with the ceremony being held on the top. Some twenty-five of them, young and old, including a few pahanas who work on the reservation, puffed into the plaza. They ran around the circle of singing women and out of the plaza. Later each was awarded a prize, in order of the finish, the first ten getting handmade baskets of coiled yucca, the others getting a container of one sort or another, even if it was a plastic garbage can. Each runner held his prize over his head and ran out of the plaza, to the applause of all except the circle of women, who, plaques in hand, kept up their song, eyes to the ground.

Footraces are a part of a number of ceremonies. The Snake Dance and the Flute Dance are preceded by dawn footraces in which men (some in their sixties and over) and boys participate. They start miles out in the plain below the mesa, exactly where the sun rises. In a sense they are running to demonstrate to the women their physical prowess and endurance. As each runner huffs and puffs into the village, the women say "*Askwali, Askwali*"—the female word for "thank you." Hopi runners are legendary: there are accounts from the turn of the century of their running 180 miles in three days in order to deliver a message.

In October the last of the corn—whatever the ravens have not managed to appropriate—is harvested. (We met one Hopi whose harvest lasted until November.) The air begins to take on a chill that even the sun, arcing to the south, cannot offset, and there is a general hunkering down. In late November there will be the Wuwutsim ceremony, the men's society ritual that initiates

The moisture in a baby's mouth, the snow melting under the feet of the Buffalo dancers, and the clouds threatening to sprinkle the Navajo dancers are all blessed.

FOLLOWING PAGES: A bride-to-be dresses her daughter in buckskin leggings on the wedding day among some of her in-laws-to-be.

Hopi men into those mysteries that lie beyond the kachina society. At such times, the village is closed off. The other religious societies take over to see that the right procedures are adhered to. The Two Horn society, the philosophers, is present, as is the One Horn society, the enforcers, who see to it that the proceedings are free of intruders. The mesas are shrouded in the cold mysteries and ordeals of winter.

The Hopi are among the most ritualistic people on earth, with much of their ancient ritual still intact. One Hopi leader speculated that the highly ritualistic nature of their lives derives from the fact that the language has until very recently been an unwritten one, that the high degree of ritual, with its constant repetition, was what made it possible to maintain the religious traditions, to keep and pass on the religious meaning of things. Yet some of the ceremonies are changing and some are dying out. Emory Sekaquaptewa told me that sometimes the Hopi people get "too creative" and a ceremony may get too elaborate, leaving behind its true purpose, which is to instill and reinforce humility among the people. When form outgrows content, when institutions have become too elaborate—and this has apparently happened often in the past—the elders have to destroy them and let humbleness and sheer survival again become the paramount goals.

In any event, some of the old ceremonies are no longer being practiced in all the villages, but these ceremonies are not the whole story. Ceremony, or ritual—with all that it implies among the Hopi, including humor and an understanding of human nature, of the forces of good and evil, and of the blessings of the earth and the sun—ceremony is part of everyday life for most Hopi we

have met, as much a regularly occurring part of existence as, say, breathing. For in the interstices of the annual ceremonial cycle (and nowadays often taking place among the responsibilities of nine-to-five jobs), there are crops to be harvested, babies to be named, craft objects to be made, couples to be wed, and all these activities—full of symbolism and spiritual content—must also be carried on properly.

Not only does everyone seem to have more than one job or task;
it seems unlikely that many Hopi could manage to live the straightforward
nine-to-five life that so many Americans do.

TASKS AND RITUALS

ON A RISE ON THE PLAIN below Shipaulovi and Mishongnovi, there is a group of buildings—some of them frame houses—that make up the Sunlight Baptist Mission, a place that seems forlorn and little-used. It is one of a handful of Christian missions sprinkled about the reservation, all of which together number about 5 percent of the Hopi among their congregations. In a dry wash behind the mission, Alonzo Quavehema maintains a cornfield, and on the dusty scrub desert between the mission and the highway there is the family's oven, a hole about seven feet deep in the hard clay. One morning late in August 1980, we went there to prepare the oven with Alonzo and his son Phillip, his daughter Darlene, and Phillip's five-year-old daughter, whom everyone called Siwa, Hopi for "youngest sister" but, on Second Mesa, used to refer to the littlest girl in the family. The hole was covered with sand piled over a couple of metal sheets; it was promptly

Widely spaced corn plants in one of Alonzo Quavehema's fields have grown well and tasseled, despite the odds against it.

opened, and Alonzo lowered himself into it and began bailing loose dirt out with a plastic bucket. Branching out from the hole, near the bottom, a tunnel ran about five feet to where it opened out on the side of an embankment. This tunnel was called the "nose" and Phillip cleared it out. We were making preparations for a corn roast, an annual event.

Once the oven and the nose were free of dirt, Alonzo began to pile brush over the hole and started a fire. Presently the burning brush fell into the oven, and Alonzo said: "Now it's alive." The rest of us piled into Phillip's truck, leaving Alonzo to tend the fire. "Usually some old man stays to watch the fire," Alonzo said, "but we couldn't find one today." Phillip made loud note of the gray in Alonzo's hair, suggesting that Alonzo would do just fine as the necessary "old man." We drove south to a field located about fifteen miles out on the desert. Along the way Phillip, an irrepressible young man in his late twenties, pointed out the buttes and other features on the horizon, telling me their Hopi names. One rounded butte had a knob on the top of it. "We call that one The Tit," said Phillip. Mother Earth, I thought.

CORN • Corn, a plant native to this hemisphere, is a central concern of the Hopi. In sandy washes apparently inhospitable to agriculture, the Hopi grow a variety of corn—each kind having symbolic as well as nutritional significance. Blue corn, for example, goes to the very origins of the Hopi, who believe that their ancestors, upon arriving in this world, were offered corn of various colors, a choice that would determine their destiny. They chose the short blue ear of corn, signifying that their life would be arduous but that they would learn to survive and would outlast all other people on this planet.

Hopi ceremonies are directed to the need for moisture for corn and other crops—melons, peaches, gourds, squash, beans—which the Hopi miraculously produce. In its turn, the corn is required to aid in the proper achievement of ceremonies.

The field was near his grandfather's sheep camp. The old man had gone there by burro to stay for months at a time every summer until he had died, the year previous. It was a long time since he had raised sheep, but he had spent much of every summer out on the desert, enjoying the solitude.

"The old man gave me this field," Phillip said, "because I would always come out and stay with him and help him with his corn." The field, about 100 yards square, was located in a depression, and we parked the pickup on a hill about 200 yards away and set out on foot down the otherwise impassable gullies, carrying large metal washtubs and gunnysacks. At the near side of the field, great tangles of melon vines lay in the sand, and Phillip stooped to untangle them. "The wind does this," he said. Some of the melons had holes in them. "And the crows do this."

Beyond the melons stood row after row of corn, all about four feet tall—squat, bushlike plants, some ten feet apart, quite unlike the close-together ranks of tall stalks that grow throughout the Midwest. Phillip explained that this whole field was Hopi sweet corn and that we were to pick it all. Every ear was to be removed from each plant—about six on the average—and the stalk stepped on so that it would lie on the ground. "It can rest. Its job is done," said Phillip.

One of the many varieties of Hopi corn is sweet corn, usually harvested by the end of August. In this sequence of photographs (through page 106), a family picks corn together, pausing in their work to playfully smear one another with corn smut, a black substance that grows on some of the ears. Smearing the corn smut is an old ritual, a roughhouse and in some cases a courtship measure.

All hands began to pick, reaching down into the tightly furled leaves to find the hard ear and twisting it off with a slight crack, feeling the moisture that the plants had miraculously extracted from deep down, below the dry sand. Susanne alternated photography with farm labor. Some of the ears had a disease called corn smut, the result of a fungus infection. The kernels affected looked like black marshmallows. Suddenly, as I was stooped over one plant, Darlene jumped on my back and smeared my face with black goo. She then went after Phillip, laughing uproariously, but he countered with his own handful of the diseased corn, and they went down in a heap. Susanne was caught and properly smeared, and Siwa's turn came.

As we were hauling our washbuckets full of corn up the hill to the truck, Phillip commented that on days when there is a corn-picking party, there might be a number of young people involved, and every now and then a guy would chase his favorite girl all over the cornfield and then out of the field and out of sight. They would come back a half hour later all smeared with the black goo. "It's a good excuse, you know," said Phillip, laughing.

By about two o'clock, after three hours of hauling the entire harvest up the hill, the back of the pickup was a foot deep in corn. We set off, Susanne electing to ride in the back with Darlene and Siwa and the corn. Phillip explained that we would dump all the corn in the oven and leave it overnight, returning at dawn to retrieve it and to have a feast.

Back at the site of the oven, Alonzo was still throwing brush into the pit. Fire flared up, and the oven made a roaring sound, just as if it were alive. Alonzo had not expected us until later, and he praised us for having picked so much

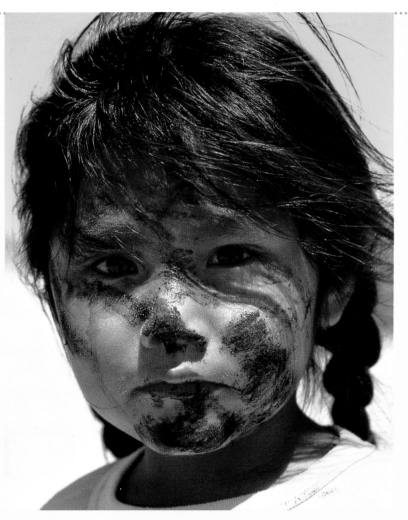

corn in so little time. As he spoke Darlene leaped on him, anointing him with black goo. He licked his lips.

"This isn't dirt, you know. It's food," he said, laughing. Indeed corn smut can be ingested without harm, but I have met Hopi who do not want to eat it.

His face blackened, Alonzo poked around in the back of Phillip's pickup, returning with two ears of corn which he proceeded to make into separate bundles with medicinal plants he had picked earlier, and tie firmly with yucca knots. "This is the Mother Corn," he said, holding up one ear, totally obscured in the bundle, "and this is the Father Corn." The second ear protruded from the bundle. "These are perfect ears of corn and they go in the oven to make it all work out right. The Mother Corn goes on the bottom, the Father Corn on the top. That's the way it always is. When you're talking about people in a family you always say the mother's name first, then the father's."

After the oven was filled, Alonzo bit a mouthful of corn from an ear he had saved and spat it into the oven; the ear was passed around and we all did the same—an act designed to help the corn cook properly. Alonzo told me to plug the nose with more husks and cover it with dirt while he and Phillip replaced the metal sheets and sealed it all with a foot of sand.

At dinner that night, sitting around the small kitchen table in Linda's house down below Shipaulovi in the new housing area, Alonzo talked of his fields. The field near the mission was not producing very well this year even though there was plenty of water. It had been his father's clan land, and therefore had not been passed on in the traditional way. Normally one derives one's fields through the mother's clan. "Maybe someone doesn't want me to be

using that field. Next year I'll just let it go." On the other hand, the field across the highway from the mission was doing fine. It had come into Linda's family when a man had wanted a "favor from a beautiful lady" in Linda's family; the favor apparently delivered, the field passed to Linda's family and eventually to Linda.

The men, she explained, own the corn that they plant and harvest until they bring it back to their wives or their mothers. Then it belongs to the women. The men build the houses for their wives, and everything inside, except for a few of the men's belongings, is the property of the women. "That's how it is out here," Linda said. "That's Phillip's corn now. Tomorrow it will be mine."

As has been stated, Hopi is a matrilineal society. One's clan derives from the mother. If one has a non-Hopi mother one cannot be a Hopi (except by adoption) even if one's father is a Hopi. While women are excluded from much of the deeper religious life of Hopi (this being the province of men), they own most property and, ever vigilant to see that things are done properly, they exert an extremely powerful influence over the men—even the priests. No one, for example, crosses the Bear Clan matriarch of a given village.

As the evening progressed, Alonzo said: "It's the Feast Moon now. This is the time of the year when everyone used to feast. The sweet corn is ripe and there are melons, squash, peaches. Everyone used to go out and harvest all that stuff and they would sit around all night feasting, and if you were walking home from your fields you sure wouldn't be hungry by the time you got home. You could stop here and there and everyone would give you something to eat. Most people don't do that anymore. It sure was fun."

RIGHT: Alonzo lifts a bucket of sand out, cleaning the pit oven.

FAR RIGHT: Alonzo stays behind, building the underground fire, while the others harvest the corn.

BELOW: Freshly picked sweet corn is shoved into the oven.

At half-past five the next morning the sun had just cleared the top of First Mesa and Antelope Mesa to the east. We found that Alonzo and Phillip had unsealed the oven. Steam rose from the dark hole, making sinuously bright forms in the first rays of the sun. Such steam is, itself, considered a prayer, evaporating into invisibility and becoming a message to the spirits. Alonzo turned to me and said: "We have to invite the spirits to come and eat with us, Jake. You call them."

Dawn is not my time of day under any circumstances. I asked Alonzo what I should say. He told me to call out and invite them however I wanted to.

"Hey, everyone, come and get it!" I shouted, feeling a bit awkward.

"That's good, that's good," Phillip said, grinning, and his father stood up near the open hole and called out in Hopi in a voice that reverberated from the crumbling sandstone edge of Second Mesa nearly a mile away. His prayer, summoning the spirits and asking them to feast with us and bless the corn, lasted for nearly a minute.

"Now," said Phillip, "the spirits are invited from all over, from all directions. If you feel something touch you, don't jump. It's a spirit." Phillip laughed. "You're going to have to learn to talk Hopi. There are a lot of things it's hard to understand in English."

Alonzo lowered himself into the hole and in seconds a plastic bucket of corn was thrust upward, to be taken and dumped on the ground by Darlene. Another and another bucket of corn emerged from the steaming pit. We began shucking the corn, some of it too hot to hold with comfort, and after several minutes Alonzo called for the ladder and returned from the underground to the pale light of dawn and the almost cloyingly sweet scent of the corn we were shucking and, from time to time, eating. Phillip descended into the pit and the process continued. It soon became my turn.

"You don't have to go down there," said Alonzo. "You'll get all dirty."

Phillip snickered. I took off some of the layers of clothes I had worn to protect me from the chill of the August dawn and dropped down into the hottest place I had ever been, standing on ears of corn and the embers of old corn husks. Phillip had explained that there is often a kind of competition to see who can stay down in the oven longest. That morning I lost the competition,

· · · · · · · · · · · · · ·

Viets Lomahaftewa looks on as his son-in-law Alfred Joshongva fashions a sash.

emerging after what seemed like an hour but was really closer to ten minutes, having contributed a fraction to the pile of corn.

By eight o'clock, and after several stints in the oven, the corn was all shucked and had been loaded into the back of the pickup. We covered the oven and drove to Linda's house and began hauling armfuls of corn into the house and dumping it on the living-room floor at Linda's feet, where she sat in an easy chair.

VILLAGE LIFE • All but one of the Hopi villages are located on three mesas—First, Second, and Third—and each mesa has different traditions and different ways of going about the daily round. Independent, yet closely knit by clan connections and largely similar traditions, the villagers enjoy the accomplishments as well as suffer the difficulties of life in an arid world. Corn and some other vegetables and fruit are grown, but paying jobs are few and houses must be refurbished; cinder block often replaces ancient stone. Many Hopi supplement their livings by making craft objects—baskets, jewelry, pottery, kachina dolls. The work of men and that of women are still precisely differentiated.

Aided by federal funds, the Hopi tribal administration was able to finance a flurry of construction in many villages in the 1970s. Hopi builders put up a new house in Mishongnovi for the Bear Clan, the clan from which the village leaders (kikmongwis) arise.

"*Askwali,*" she said, as each armful came through the door, "*askwali.*" It was now her corn and she would spend the rest of the day and part of the night stringing the ears on wire so that they could be hung up on the outside of her house to dry. As the winter came and went, she would plunge some of the dry brown ears into boiling water and it would become moist again and taste as sweet as it had when we were shucking it.

Alonzo left almost immediately after the corn had been delivered. He was late, but he had received permission from the school he worked at to be late so that this task could be completed. The Bureau of Indian Affairs, ultimately Alonzo's employer, has come a long way, at least locally. Today they recognize the value of Hopi ways—the requirement that such simple day-to-day events as corn roasts take place, events whose tradition calls for things to be done in a certain ceremonial way, a ceremonial way that is considerate of the needs of the spirits as well as mindful of the fundamental biological nature of humanity.

The Hopi world is a church, and the Hopi church is a community of all the ways of being human, including the ribald and the spiritual. And to this day the Sunlight Baptist Mission, brooding implausibly among the folds and bulges of the geological detritus of Second Mesa, seems to me, however well-meant, a little silly, a reminder of the confusion with which the white world has so often looked upon the Hopi mesas, seeking either to replace their rich and fecund tradition with its own theology or to "improve" an economy that has lasted for a millennium.

The Hopi Reservation is under the ultimate jurisdiction of the federal government, whose obligations are discharged by the Secretary of the Interior through the Commissioner of Indian Affairs, heading the Bureau of Indian Affairs. Since 1975 the local superintendent of the BIA, located in Keams Canyon, to the east of the Hopi mesas, has been Alph Secakuku, a Hopi; this makes the Hopi Reservation one of two in the nation whose superintendents are of the same tribe as the people being administered. And the Hopi police force, administratively a child of the BIA, has for the last several years had a Hopi police chief. A young man from First Mesa, Ivan Sidney had always wanted to be a policeman, and as a young adult he decided that he would pursue that career even though it precluded his following the path into one or another of the priesthoods. He joined the state police and before he was thirty was appointed chief of the Hopi police. During the late seventies, he built up the force, training the Hopi and other Indian men who served on it into an efficient and unique cadre. In 1977 the Hopi police had the best conviction record of any Indian police force in the country. That was because Sidney had, among other things, spent so much time teaching his men to fill out reports of arrests in such a way that they would hold up in court. Sidney also trained his men in SWAT techniques so that they could scale cliffs and chase down in the night the pothunters who seek to make a profit from artifacts in the myriad old ruins and cemeteries that dot the Hopi landscape. In late 1981, Sidney was elected Tribal Chairman.

The main complexity for the Hopi police is the plethora of laws—both white and Hopi—which they must enforce. On days when a ceremony is taking place in one of the villages, the Hopi police are always present. But they are not there really as representatives of the federal government or as enforcers of federal law or state law or county law. They are not there to do the bidding of the Hopi

Tribal Council or even of the village chief, or kikmongwi. For when a ceremony takes place in a village it is the leader of that ceremony who is in charge. The police take their orders from him. It has not always been so, but today the Hopi police respond to the Hopi way of life as well as to the imposed laws of white civilization, though I have heard a few complaints that they are a bit too tough on Hopi people caught speeding or in other infractions (the most frequent of which is the possession of alcohol, a federal offence). Today, more often than not, the individual policemen are given time off so that they can be at ceremonies at their villages, be it a kachina dance or one of the many other ceremonies with which Hopi life is filled.

It has been said that the Hopi have in the past few decades changed from a subsistence economy, in which growing crops was the main sustenance of most people, mixed with a bit of the white man's cash economy (that is, paying jobs), to a cash economy mixed with a little bit of subsistence agriculture. Such a shift is certainly putting a strain on traditional Hopi ways, which are so closely tied to the daily requirements of agriculture and ritual. The changeover began in earnest in 1950, when Congress passed the Navajo–Hopi Settlement Act, which brought nearly $90 million to this corner of the Southwest for the building of roads, digging of wells, and other construction providing work for local people. About 1,000 Hopi live off the reservation, working at a variety of jobs in such cities as Winslow, Flagstaff, and Phoenix, generally returning for important ceremonies—and almost always returning for good after retirement. A considerable number on the reservation are employed by the tribal administration, the BIA, and the occasional local construction job.

Royalties amounting to some $500,000 a year from the Peabody Coal Company mine on the north end of Black Mesa supply income for the tribal administration that enables it to hire Hopi people to provide the customary social services and also to administer the various job-training and other programs funded by the federal government, either directly or through the BIA. Among the facilities on the reservation is a Public Health Service (PHS) hospital located in Keams Canyon, staffed by a remarkably dedicated group of doctors (mostly white) and nurses and technicians (mostly Hopi); it serves not only the Hopi people but many nearby Navajo. It can supply basic medical care, but cases requiring complicated surgery or the attention of a specialist are flown to the PHS hospital in Phoenix or Tuba City. Every week a small plane ferries such patients, flying from a single strip located across the highway from, and west of, Polacca.

The Hopi Community Services facility, chiefly a school for the few mentally and physically handicapped individuals on the reservation, a lonely group of buildings where Hopi personnel (for the most part) provide special education and care, is located about ten miles down the road toward Winslow. Many of the very elderly were, in recent times, shipped off to nursing homes in Winslow and Phoenix, but this practice seems to be losing favor with the Hopi, and more often than not a Hopi dies with dignity in the family home.

To cope with fire, an omnipresent danger at Hopi, as anywhere else, there is a fire department located in Keams Canyon, a good thirty miles from, say, Kykotsmovi. Virtually all these services are federally funded. This of course may change. In 1981, an editorial in the Hopi newspaper *Qua Tokti (Cry of the*

BELOW LEFT: The sure hands of Victor Coochwytewa, a leading Hopi silversmith, cut a traditional pattern from a disk of silver for an overlay brooch.

RIGHT: In his workshop near Hotevilla, on Third Mesa, with his talented niece, Verma Nequatewa (Sonwai), as co-worker, the internationally known jeweler Charles Loloma takes Hopi tradition a step beyond, using a variety of materials to create jewelry that reflects the soul of the wearer.

Eagle), which is privately owned, warned that the new federal administration's budget-cutting would lead to the shutdown of a great many services and the loss of many jobs on the reservation. Perhaps, the editorial suggested, this was not all bad. Perhaps it would send the Hopi back into the bountiful ways of old, when people had to rely upon each other and the land for their livelihood.

Many Hopi elders have long looked askance at the growing influence of the federal government, arising out of its prominent role in providing employment and services on the reservation. They have said for a long time that the federal government would not always be there to help; ancient suspicions die hard. And of course the elders' prophecies are being borne out. A new federal administration has cut many programs that affect the Hopi (and the other Indian people). Public Health Service employees are now in many cases working only thirty-two hours a week—or at least that is all they are paid for. Health services are thus diminished. The PHS hospital can no longer provide medicine free, so that many Hopi now go without the medicine the doctors at the hospital prescribe. Jobs and job training are in shorter supply. Some services, such as the Hopi police, will not grow, as had been hoped, but will continue at current levels. All in all, signs point to a considerable amount of personal hardship for the sick and elderly and a thinning of opportunity for younger Hopi, which they resent. The elders, however, have always said that life would not be easy and that it was necessary to confront hardship, and they see this new budgetary environment as an opportunity for the Hopi to regain the independence and self-sufficiency they enjoyed for centuries before becoming spoiled by federal handouts.

There is little of what white people would call private enterprise on the reservation. In Polacca a tiny outfit employs a few men and women to make electronic parts for Hewlett-Packard under a contract. The Hopi Cultural Center is owned by the tribe, but its daily operation of motel and restaurant services is franchised out to a Hopi couple. The Second Mesa store, which sells groceries, hardware, and livestock feed, is privately owned by Hopi. There is a used-car lot below First Mesa, and there are a few gas stations and auto repair shops owned by Hopi dotted here and there along Route 264. There used to be two Laundromats in Kykotsmovi, but one closed down, and the other never seems to be open or operative. For much of their shopping and laundry and so forth the Hopi drive to Winslow, or, if they live on Third Mesa, to Flagstaff.

The trading posts, one at each mesa (the one at Third Mesa is owned by the Babbitt family, which has also supplied Arizona with its governor), are generally small and therefore the prices are high. Ferrell Secakuku, who owns the Second Mesa trading post, has long dreamed of turning his store into a kind of mini-shopping mall with a supermarket and Laundromat and other facilities, so that he could bring his food prices down and make the long trips to Winslow and Flagstaff unnecessary for many people. But a point of Hopi tradition made this project controversial and delayed it for many years. Ferrell's mother came from the village of Bacabi, and although she moved out early on, owing to a family altercation, and lived with Ferrell's father on Second Mesa, where he started the store, many people on Second Mesa say that Ferrell should have grown up in Bacabi, since a man traditionally moves to his wife's village. Furthermore, since Ferrell's wife, Dorothy, comes from First Mesa, people say he should have

moved there, and they have strenuously opposed his attempts to enlarge the store despite the probable benefits to the Hopi. In late 1981, after several years of bickering, he simply took matters into his own hands and began building a far larger store behind the pleasantly ramshackle one. It opened in early 1982.

Where the Hopi meet the marketplace on their own terms and with great success is in crafts. There is a young man who works in the Hopi Cultural Center as general handyman. He also sits in from time to time as a disc jockey in a nearby city and has regularly won most of the disco contests put on by the Catholic Church in Keams Canyon. But his chief occupation is art: he paints large canvases in black and white—great heads of people that look very Hopi, very thoughtful.

"Everyone here," he said to Susanne, "is creative. Everyone is making something. Take a look at the guy in the restaurant. He's a busboy and everyone probably looks at him and says, yeah, there's an Indian working as a busboy. What they don't realize is that he's also a jeweler. A silversmith."

Hopi silver craft characteristically employs the technique known as silver overlay. To make an overlay belt buckle, for example, the silversmith cuts out two identical rectangles from a thin sheet of silver. On one of the pieces he etches a design and then, with a jeweler's saw, cuts out the design. Next, he solders the piece with the design cut out of it to the other piece. The front of the combined piece is treated with an acidic solution that oxidizes it and turns it black. The silversmith then buffs and polishes the surface until it gleams, except for the recessed design, which remains black.

Hopi overlay is not an ancient craft. Until the 1930s there were only a few Hopi silversmiths, and most of them worked in the design tradition of the Navajo

NEAR RIGHT: A Third Mesa craftsman paints a recently completed figure.

FAR RIGHT: A Hotevilla grandfather, Percy Lomaquahu, weaves a bride's robe.

BELOW: The jewelry of Charles Loloma brought about a whole new style featured by Tiffany & Co. and emulated by many other jewelers from other tribes.

and Zuni, with inlaid stones such as turquoise and coral and design stamped into the silver. What may be the earliest Hopi overlay bracelet dates back to 1939–40. It was designed by Virgil Hubert, of the Museum of Northern Arizona in Flagstaff, and executed by a Hopi named Pierce Kywanwytewa. It is now in the Museum's collection—appropriately, since it was Mary-Russell Ferrell Colton, founder (with her husband, Harold Colton) of the Museum, who originally encouraged the Hopi to use the technique of overlay and, by adopting designs similar to those found on traditional Hopi pottery, to create a unique style. After World War II, a number of returning Hopi veterans formed a craft guild and learned the technique. Currently the guild comprises more than thirty silversmiths and there are more than a hundred others working elsewhere, on and off the reservation.

Demand for Hopi silverwork is high and the prices are commensurate, particularly since the price of silver (which is bought on the open market) has skyrocketed. Pieces by some of the more widely known jewelers, such as Victor Coochwytewa and Charles Loloma (who works in a nontraditional contemporary style), sell for thousands of dollars.

Another craft that is practiced by men in all villages on the reservation is the carving of kachina dolls. They are made from the roots of cottonwood trees, most often of several pieces glued together, and are elaborately painted and decorated. There are several hundred kachinas in the Hopi pantheon, and the dolls vary widely in quality and price—ranging from simple to extremely intricate, and from $50 to more than $1,000. A group of young carvers, among them Lowell Talashoma of Shipaulovi and Wilford Duwyenke of Kykotsmovi, have taken to making their dolls out of one piece of wood and painstakingly carving

Some superior carvers, like Lowell Talashoma (*left*), make their entire living from their craft. Talashoma is one of the few new-generation carvers who make their dolls whole, out of one piece of wood. Most Hopi men carve kachina dolls, using the roots of cottonwood trees. They often supplement their incomes by carving dolls for sale. The dolls teach children to distinguish between the kachinas and understand the role of these spirit messengers.

BELOW: Crow Mother kachina represents a key Bean Dance figure.

all the details (for example, carving feathers rather than gluing real ones on) and also leaving certain parts of the dolls unpainted. The effects of what might be called a new realism are stunning, but there are those who prefer the spirited effect of the more "naive" dolls.

Just when the Hopi began making kachina dolls is not clear. During the excavation of part of Walpi for a restoration project carried out there as part of the nation's Bicentennial, a highly simplified doll, little more than a flat board with a head carved on one end, was found. It was dated to the late nineteenth century; a doll in the Smithsonian dates back to the 1880s. The practice may have begun earlier, though, for even in the arid climate of the mesas wooden artifacts tend to succumb to the elements.

Kachina dolls were, formerly, to be played with. Emory Sekaquaptewa told us how, in his childhood, he would see old battered and broken kachina dolls in dumps, discarded the way the white culture discards its toys—except that the Hopi thought of this as mirroring the life cycle: you are born, you live a while, you go back to the earth. Now they are considered by most Hopi children as too valuable to be played with, and they wind up mounted on the walls of the girls' homes.

Another craft practiced only by men is weaving. Men weave the white cotton robes for brides, the traditional black dresses (*mantas*), and various sashes and belts—usually created for ceremonial purposes but in a few instances for sale—in particular, traditional black belts with green and red designs woven in. The men also do the knitting, making black leggings that are used in certain ceremonies. Most of these items are made from cotton yarn or string bought outside, but traditionally the Hopi grew their own cotton. When the Spanish

In the villages of Third Mesa, the women specialize in weaving plaques and baskets not of yucca but of multicolored wicker. These have ceremonial uses and are also made for the craft market. Like the coiled yucca plaques of Second Mesa, they often incorporate symbols of kachinas, the sun, clouds, and other natural phenomena. Indeed, rarely is a Hopi craft object merely an attractive design executed in a particular style; all depict something considered important to the maker.

BELOW: Anna Lomaquahu from Hotevilla at work.

arrived in the sixteenth century, they found the Hopi wearing white skirts much like the kilts still seen in ceremonies.

Hopi farmers used to grow cotton plants here and there, wherever there was a likelihood of a fair amount of water. Over the years they would collect the cotton and keep it against the day when they would have to weave a wedding robe for one of their sons. When that time came, they would distribute bits of the cotton to everyone in the village, seeking their help in taking all the seeds out so that the cotton could be spun. The people who helped with this task would be paid back in due course with food and other gifts.

Hopi craftswomen tend to specialize—by mesa. On Third Mesa the women make a circular plaque (*hungyapu*) from wicker. Such plaques are often multicolored and bear a traditional symbol, such as an eagle or a crow bride; also used are more abstract symbols, denoting, for example, the descent of the spirit after death to the Underworld.

On Second Mesa, the women make a round coiled plaque (*poota*) by wrapping thin bundles of yucca tightly with yucca strips that have been dyed four colors—black, green, yellow, red (and occasionally brown). On both Third and Second Mesa, the women employ their special techniques to make baskets as well.

On First Mesa the women's craft is pottery. Throughout the mesa's villages the visitor finds signs in the windows and on the doors—"Pottery for Sale." Hopi pottery is made without benefit of the potter's wheel; it is molded by hand from local clays, sometimes from coils of clay. Once it dries, the maker polishes the pot with a stone and then paints it, using a thick strip of yucca as a paint-

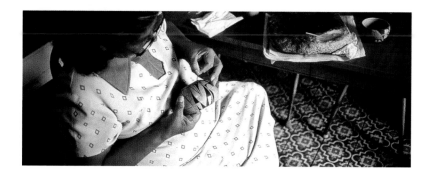

Pottery is the specialty on First Mesa. Bowls, jugs, and vases of various shapes are formed from local clay. The characteristic curvilinear designs derive from ancient pottery patterns rediscovered in the late nineteenth century when archaeologists were excavating a Hopi ruin near First Mesa. After nearly a hundred years, these patterns seem once again to be second nature to First Mesa potters; not surprisingly, most of them are symbolic of rain and its associated phenomena—lightning, clouds, and wind. Norma Ami (*left*) of Middle Village, First Mesa, a prolific potter, made the pot shown below.

brush and paints made by mixing local earths with water. When the paint is dry, the potter builds a small bed of sheep dung out on the edge of the mesa, places the pots on it and surrounds them with yet more sheep dung (which, by the way, is usually purchased from Navajo people), and sets the pile on fire. After about three hours, the fire dies out and the pottery is finished.

The design of Hopi pottery is not a continuous tradition. After the arrival of the Spaniards in the sixteenth century, Hopi pottery for some reason entered on a long period of artistic decline. The designs were cramped and formal, whereas earlier they had been free in form, bold, exuberant. Toward the end of the nineteenth century, the archaeologist J. W. Fewkes began the excavation of Sikyatki, an old ruin located north of the present First Mesa villages; one Hopi employed at the dig was married to a woman named Nampeyo, from the First Mesa village of Hano. Fascinated by the old designs on the pottery that came to light, she began to use them on her own pottery, initiating a neoclassical revival which caught on immediately and is the source of the style used to this day on First Mesa. Nampeyo's daughters, granddaughters, and great-granddaughters—and an exception to the rule, one grandson (who also works as a ranger for the tribal administration)—are among the best Hopi potters.

A great-great-grandson of Nampeyo is one of the finest painters the Hopi have produced—Dan Namingha, whose mammoth mural, an abstract rendering of First Mesa and the desert below, hangs prominently in the Phoenix airport. Namingha's work is shown in galleries in Santa Fe and Scottsdale and has been exhibited in several Western museums as well as in Europe. Five other Hopi artists, including Milland Lomakema, whose drawings appear on these

pages, banded together several years ago to form an organization called Artist Hopid. Their works are a major feature of the Hopi museum located in the Hopi Cultural Center, on Second Mesa, and have been widely exhibited throughout the West. They formed the group, a kind of cooperative, in order to gain better control over their market, but there was more to it than that. As one

Milland Lomakema (*below*) is proud to be the Hopi's "most artistic bureaucrat." His creation painting is at right. At far right is a kachina maiden by Dan Namingha. Namingha (*below right*), of First Mesa, is the great-great-grandson of the most famous Hopi potter, Nampeyo. He combines Hopi themes with his own mystical visions, and though he has studied at Chicago's American Academy of Art and elsewhere, he says, "All my ideas evolve from my heritage and from the things I have seen and experienced."

of the members, Michael Kabotie, wrote: "We, the Hopis, have a lot to offer from a spiritual standpoint and as a living force. And we are hoping that from the preservation of our traditions, and from the interpretations of the Hopi way in our art and paintings, a new direction can come for American spirituality." Most of the Artist Hopid paintings depict ceremonial events or events from the Hopi creation story or the gathering of the clans. There are, for most Hopi artists, few other worthy themes.

This spiritual urge is common among Hopi artists and craftsmen. Lowell Talashoma, the kachina doll carver of Shipaulovi, lived for most of his youth off the reservation, and he attributes his desire and his ability to carve representations of the kachina spirits to a spiritual reawakening he experienced upon returning and involving himself in ceremonial life. Charles Loloma, the internationally known jeweler of Hotevilla, likes to inlay the inside of bracelets or rings

with turquoise or lapis, signifying that the wearer's soul is known only to the wearer. Most Hopi jewelers employ the traditional designs in their work—clan symbols, cloud symbols, all reminders of Hopi religion.

Few of the Hopi craftspeople and artists fully support themselves by their efforts; most take other jobs as well to make ends meet. Milland Lomakema, for example, was employed by the tribal administration; this made him, in his words, "the Hopi's most artistic bureaucrat." Virtually everyone at Hopi does more than one thing, has more than one task. Norma Renee, a grandmother who lives in Sichomovi (more often called Middle Village), supplements her Social Security payments by being a potter, and she is also a healer. Like most Hopi healers, Norma is a specialist; she concentrates on diagnosing and setting broken bones. One day a young boy in her village fell and hurt his arm. X-rays taken at the hospital in Keams Canyon were negative, and a painkiller was prescribed. He

continued to complain, and the next day his mother took him to Norma. She held his arm for a few minutes and then drew a line on his forearm with a ballpoint pen. "Take him back to Keams," she instructed, "and have them look there." This time the X-ray showed a hairline fracture exactly under Norma's line.

Some healers work in close cooperation with the PHS doctors, who have learned that the Hopi healers are capable of certain kinds of psychosomatic healing that are helpful when used alongside their own medicine. The healers and their patients know that there is a great deal more involved than psychological persuasion.

While much of Hopi healing is psychic in nature, straightforward herbal medicine is widely practiced, and the Hopi pharmacopoeia is vast. Having lived in one area so long, the Hopi are well aware of the healing powers of its various plants. For example, Hopi tea, which grows wild here and there on the desert and along the roadsides, is very soothing for an upset stomach. Alonzo Quavehema once pointed out a plant, apparently a kind of aster, flowering along the road, and said it provided Hopi birth control. Boiled in water and drunk regularly by a woman after childbirth, it would apparently prolong the period when she could not conceive. The pungent root of a shrub with reddish bark, resembling ironwood—called bear root or in Hopi *honnyaapi*—is good for a sore throat and several other afflictions. It wards off evil spirits and can be used—along with certain mysterious rites—to eliminate the effects of some kinds of witchcraft.

Hopi healers never charge for their services. A woman healer we know has found herself inundated not only with Hopi patients but with Navajo patients as well and is desperately seeking some polite way to restrict her practice to Hopi, there being only so many hours in the day and the Hopi being, of course, her first priority.

Not only does everyone seem to have more than one job or task; it seems unlikely that many Hopi could manage to live the straightforward nine-to-five life that so many Americans do. The ceremonial cycle intervenes throughout the year with a regular beat and an interminable number of tasks and obligations. Each ceremony can occupy a large number of people for a long time.

For nineteen days after a baby is born it is kept out of the direct view of the sun. A few days before the baby naming, the traditional Hopi stew is prepared at the home of the infant's maternal grandmother. Well before dawn on the last day, the baby's paternal aunts, from young girls to elderly women, make their way through the dark and begin to trickle into the grandmother's house. While a child belongs to its mother's clan, it is named for its father's clan. People sit around chatting while the grandmother bustles about.

Presently the baby is brought forth, wrapped in a blanket. The grandmother kneels on the floor and washes the mother's hair, then unwraps the baby and bathes it in a pan of water on the floor, wrapping it up again in the blanket so that only its head protrudes. With a perfectly formed ear of corn—the baby's Mother Corn—she rubs a mixture of cornmeal and water on the baby's hair, dipping the corn in the liquid and applying it four times. The same rite is performed in turn by each of the baby's paternal aunts. Each person present gives the baby a gift, usually a new blanket, and each aunt suggests a name for the child, based on the father's clan. Thus a child whose father is of the Coyote Clan might receive a name (one word) that means the graceful turning of a coyote as it pauses and looks back at you.

LEFT: Before dawn of the infant's twentieth day, the baby's hair is ritually washed, its face is dusted with sacred cornmeal, and it is ritually blessed with Mother Corn. (Later it receives its name outdoors in presentation to the rising sun.)

BELOW: Some Hopi babies spend their early days in cradleboards.

Another suggested name might mean the manner in which butterflies flutter around a corn plant just after it has rained. Of all the names proposed, the grandmother chooses one, and as dawn approaches, she takes some cornmeal outside and sprinkles it in four lines on the ground and she sets out a plate of food for the sun. And just as the sun shows its forehead over the horizon, the grandmother takes the baby outside, bundled in its myriad blankets, and introduces it to the god.

After the baby returns from its meeting with the sun, it is temporarily ignored while a tablecloth is spread out on the floor and food in great quantities is brought out—Hopi bread, *piki, noqkwivi,* chiles, little balls of blue-cornmeal pudding wrapped in corn husks, and coffee. A first wave of aunts kneel or sit around the cloth on the floor and feast while others wait their turn and still others—friends of the family—arrive to partake of the food and wish the baby well. They sit on the floor to eat in the manner of the old days, in order to be closer to those who once lived on that spot but who have passed on.

Later in life when the child is initiated, the name it received as a baby will have another one added to it, in a sense denoting a new birth. Nowadays neither of these names is used much in public. Formerly teachers in the BIA schools gave children Christian names. These days each child is given a Christian name by its parents and it takes its father's last name, and thus named it confronts the greater world.

Relatively speaking, naming a baby is a simple ceremony; a wedding is highly complex and may take years to accomplish. Courtship could be described as recently as fifty years ago as a rather formalized series of procedures which began with a rabbit hunt. The Hopi hunted rabbits on foot, killing them

with a boomerang with sharpened edges, in the use of which they could be highly proficient (many still are). Young women went with the men on the hunt, and when a rabbit was killed they all ran for it, the first to arrive claiming it and giving the boomerang thrower some cornmeal cakes (called *somioki*) in return. At the day's end each girl was free to give somioki to whichever boy she particularly liked. A young man so favored would take the cakes to his parents and find out if they had any objections to the girl. (If the parents objected, the rejected girl apparently had the option of making some piki and bringing it to them; they would then have to accept her out of fear that she might be "more than human," that is, a witch.) A few days later the girl would set about grinding corn; the boy would visit her in her parents' home and courtship would begin. In any event, as the courtship proceeded, the young woman would pass piki out to all the male relatives of the groom-to-be, putting them in a "trap." These men would have to begin thinking about where the cotton would come from for the bride's wedding robes, since the groom's clan uncles were responsible for weaving them.

Soon after these preliminaries, the wedding ceremony would take place and the couple would go to live in the bride's mother's house for one year, the groom planting his own cornfield and one for his mother-in-law.

Courtship practices appear to be becoming far less formalized and more in keeping with those of white culture. More often than not, the couple is married in church or in town, to satisfy the state and Social Security regulations. Then they simply find a place to live and move in while the ceremonial wheels are slowly grinding. Not all the men, for example, know how to weave now, so that it may

take a long time, years even, for the groom's uncles to come forth with the robes for the bride. And by the time they have been made, there are often children of the union; a daughter of the bride must also have a robe woven for her, delaying matters yet further. Meanwhile, the bride and her family must be preparing things

LEFT and BELOW: A raucous part of every Hopi wedding is when there is an outbreak among the maternal and paternal aunts, decrying or defending the quality of the couple and attacking one another with four colors of mud.

RIGHT: A bride and her daughter in wedding robes. The bride holds her shroud, woven by her father-in-law, in rolled-up reeds called a "suitcase."

to pay back the groom's family for the robes—for example, on Second Mesa this will call for large numbers of coiled plaques to be made and held in readiness, as well as prodigious amounts of food. In the old days, the bride's family would grind 800 to 1,000 pounds of corn in a few days for this purpose.

However, in many—probably most—Hopi weddings a great many of the traditional customs are still observed. For example, four days before the wedding the bride goes to her mother-in-law's house and grinds corn from dawn to dark, customarily talking only with the mother-in-law, fasting, and preparing the family's meals without advice as a test of her ability. During this four-day period, and usually on the day before the wedding itself, a kind of war is declared by the groom's aunts. The paternal aunts, who, by clan relationship, have been very close to the groom from birth—in a sense, a vast band of sweethearts or girlfriends—prefer to think that the bride is nowhere near good enough for their darling. Young and old, they charge up to the house where the bride is grinding corn, to be met by the groom's maternal aunts, of a similar array of ages. There ensues a melee of insults and actual mudslinging; the women carry buckets of slimy mud, which they spread all over each other, rubbing each other's hair in it, attacking and counterattacking. All the while, the groom's paternal aunts shout that the bride is too fat, a terrible cook, frigid, and no doubt barren, while the other side protests and accuses the groom of almost total inadequacy. Often the groom's father will turn up, only to be attacked, stripped, covered with mud, and to have his hair cut (according to one Hopi, a vestige of the oldtime practice of scalping). This is all carried out with considerable physical vigor—old women falling to the ground only to scramble up to

rejoin the fray—and with general hilarity. After about twenty minutes the mock battle, or raid, is over and everyone goes into the mud-smeared house, where the bride is still patiently grinding corn. All carry huge armfuls of food—traditional Hopi food mixed with bags of store-bought flour and soft drinks—out to their pickups and take it home with them. The battle between the aunts is said to provide a forum where in-law antagonisms are acted out once and for all, and the mud, made of course with water, symbolizes the importance of that essential element in Hopi life.

LEFT: A procession of relatives, bearing food, follows the bride to her mother's house.

BELOW: At the Home Dance in July, the bride is presented to the kachinas, a solemn occasion when the bride in her robes may not smile.

On the day of the actual wedding ceremony the mother-in-law dresses the bride's hair in the matronly style—that is, hanging loose or in braids. Traditionally all Hopi maidens wore their hair wound into two large whorls, one on each side, but this time-consuming hairdo is used now only on ceremonial occasions. The groom's parents make a kind of shampoo from yucca roots and wash the couple's hair and, after a solemn speech by an elder describing the sacred duty of the wife to be good until the day she dies, during which the entire extended family gathered in the house weep copiously, the couple is pronounced married. A procession of relatives carries food to the bride's mother's house, and a feast ensues. The wedding is an extremely solemn occasion; throughout it, and any time the woman dons her wedding robes again, for whatever reason, she must not smile.

The robes consist of a large garment woven tightly out of white cotton, from the corners of which tassels hang, and a smaller one, also with tassels, which the bride carries rolled up in a reed scroll called in English a "suitcase." The tassels hanging down symbolize rain. Some tassels have symbolic representations of corn woven into them, some have a series of canes diminishing in length. The canes represent the woman's life course; she will bend toward the earth as she gets older. If she continues to lead a proper life through all her days, fulfilling all the ceaseless duties and traditional obligations of day-to-day life, she will reach the point where the last and shortest cane is used—whereupon her forehead will touch the ground and she will die. When, in July, all the previous brides are presented to the kachinas at the Home Dance, standing, with eyes cast down, behind their mothers-in-law, it is this ultimate goal that is being rehearsed.

And when the woman dies, she will be wrapped in the robe that she has kept throughout her life in the "suitcase," and she will be as pure again and as young as when she was married. She will stand on the edge of Grand Canyon. She will spread her robe and step onto it and descend like a white cloud to the home of Hopi souls.

PASSAGES • Hopi life is full of passages, rites, and ordeals signaling a new status in society. All these passages, all these stages, are thought of as a continuum, a kind of circle. A traditional wedding, for example, involves a great many clan and kin relations, each carrying out a number of prescribed obligations. Because some of these are arduous, a Hopi wedding may take years to accomplish, during which time the couple may have produced several children. Each of these is included in the ceremony.

A Hopi wedding is a solemn occasion, centering on the bride, her own clan, and the clan relatives of her husband. The Hopi bride wears specially created robes, and when thus attired she may not smile. In all its aspects the wedding is, in a sense, a rehearsal for the rest of the bride's life—at the end of which she will rejoin the world of the spirits. The children, as they are born, must also be presented properly to the world of relatives, spirits, and gods. A newborn Hopi must not see the sun until the twentieth day of its life. That day, at dawn, the child is taken out to see the rising sun, a reciprocal introduction, and named.

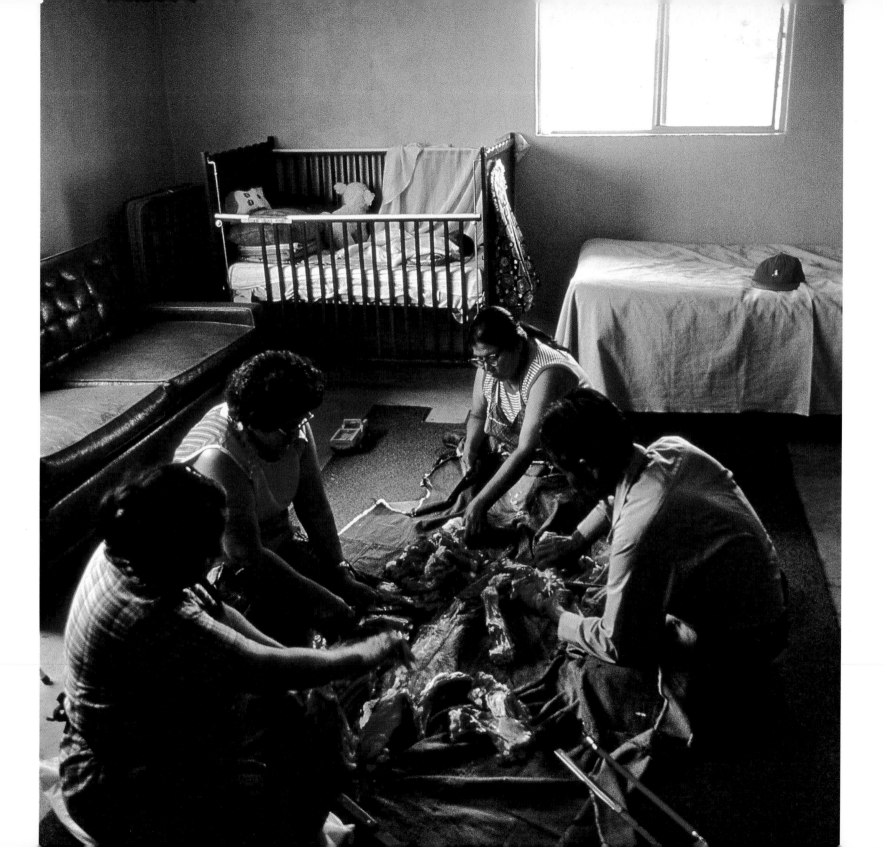

For whites it is almost axiomatic that not to know the past is to be condemned to repeat it; in contrast, one might say that for Hopi not to know their past is to be condemned *not* to repeat it.

PASTS

AMONG HOPI THE PAST is current events. In a sense, every Hopi is a historian, passionately concerned with his or her origins and the potentials and limitations specified therein. And at Hopi every clan has its own particular history.

Each clan arrived on the Hopi mesas after a long, ordeal-filled series of adventures, migrating by a preordained plan, and each clan today keeps track of its own history, its own migration story. Hopi history is chiefly an oral affair, with stories of amazing detail being passed on from clan uncle to nephew, aunt to niece, over generations. The details vary from clan to clan; one gets the sense that Hopi history is different in purpose from the body of knowledge that white historians and archaeologists seek to build up. History,

Beside the trail that leads from the Hopi mesas to an ancient shrine where salt was gathered in the Grand Canyon, a large boulder bears the markings of clans that carved their emblems into the rock each time they passed on a pilgrimage.

as white culture practices it, is linear—a ribbon-like series of events, one following another from some point in the past up to the present. It is full of gaps that historians try to fill in by finding new written or physical evidence.

For whites it is almost axiomatic that not to know the past is to be condemned to repeat it; in contrast, one might say that for Hopi not to know their past is to be condemned *not* to repeat it—to have, in fact, no idea who they are. In a sense that may be astonishing to members of the white culture, Hopi history is the essence of the present, a highly personal matter that serves to locate a Hopi in the universe.

Social scientists and historians look for verifiable evidence of events having taken place in a continuum: out of such chronological accounts certain patterns may arise and meaning can logically be adduced. Since Hopi people all know the meaning of their past, they are less concerned with exact chronologies and precise dates. Events occur *because of* meaning, not the other way around.

LEFT: An unusual kachina doll, shown ascending the ladder from a kiva, and a scary one associated with the ogres.

BELOW RIGHT: Can you identify this familiar figure that has appeared throughout this book?

Another indication of the difference between the approach of the Hopi to the past and that of white culture, by and large, is the search for roots that is currently fashionable in America. Genealogies become important: one traces one's lineage back to pre-Jamestown names in England, or wherever. Hopi do not merely have lineages; they have clans. Given a few generations, lineages begin to mean a lot less than clans. It is your Hopi clan that has a story that is relevant to the present; the clan has meaning in a social context over time. To be a part of the Eagle Clan, for example, is to know something about your place in the world, where you came from and what your proper role is, to be part of a distinct social reality that has always existed. That is very different from tracing a path— wedding by wedding—back to some ancient union and seeing yourself as the latest in a long chain of genetically connected postage stamps.

In this the Hopi are lucky. Unlike many other groups, Indian and non-Indian, in our society, they never lost sight of their roots. To ask a Hopi if he knew his roots would cause a look of polite puzzlement, just as if you were to suggest that a corn plant could grow in thin air without being attached to the earth.

We began to realize the difference when one day we were invited to accompany George Nasafti, the Bluebird Clan leader from Shungopavi, on a trip to see two old Hopi ruins, Wupatki and Tuzigoot. As an elder of the clan responsible for Hopi history, George spent much of his time in the past, going over and over in his mind his uncles' stories of the gathering of the clans. Though the ruins (both located southwest of Hopi) were important in his clan's migration story, he had never seen them. Both had been excavated and partly restored earlier in the century by the National Park Service.

The Bear Clan, George told us, had lived for a time at Wupatki, which is north and east of San Francisco Peaks, before migrating to the mesas, whither it was followed by several associated clans, including the Bluebird Clan. It was at Wupatki that a curious event had taken place, George's uncles had told him. The men, instead of praying assiduously for rain, had begun spending most of their time gambling and playing ball games. In a Hopi version of *Lysistrata* the women had grown disgusted. They ignored the men and built a tunnel from the Bear Clan house to their own underground kiva, so that they could go back and forth without seeing the discredited men. Thus, George said, arose the Marau ceremony, one of the women's dances, which is still performed in behalf of the fertility of the land. In this matrilineal society, the women take charge even of day-to-day matters if the men fail.

Wupatki (the name means "tall house") is one of the four restored ruins in the Wupatki National Monument. It is perched on a knoll overlooking a valley within sight of the brilliantly colored summit of the volcano called Sunset Crater. On the valley floor is a round stonemasonry ball court, one of two in northern Arizona, and nearer to the ruin is what looks like an open-air amphitheater, the remains of a kiva. The ruin itself consists of a long, narrow collection of old stone houses, some two stories high, most now roofless.

As we approached, George said, "Good, there is the Bear Clan house. That's where the chief lived. There is the kiva. It doesn't have its roof on anymore. But where's the tunnel? My uncles told me there should be a tunnel." George, a small man even by Hopi standards, bustled back and forth and then began to dig in the dirt with his hands. "It should be right here," he said, throwing aside

dirt and rocks until he found some old stonework. "There it is," he said, satisfied. "The archaeologist didn't find it. They should have talked to *me*."

What the archaeologists say about Wupatki is that by about A.D. 600 a people called the Sinagua moved into the area around San Francisco Peaks, locating their homes—partly underground dwellings called pit houses—near the old cinder fields, which were the best places for growing crops. In 1065 the last of the local volcanoes erupted, leaving Sunset Crater and sending fiery globs of molten lava, cinders, and ash up into the sky to fall, under the sway of the prevailing southwesterly winds, to the northeast, burying some of the pit houses as the people fled. Timbers from the pit houses have provided the annual tree-ring record by which the eruption has been dated. But the porous material falling to the earth provided excellent mulch that held the limited moisture in the ground, and soon people returned to enjoy the improved farmland. It was then, in the 1100s, that Wupatki and some of the other villages in the area were established, Wupatki expanding to more than 100 rooms, with some buildings three stories high. In 1215 a severe drought began, and by 1225 the villages were ghost towns.

Leaving Wupatki ourselves, we drove south for an hour or so to Tuzigoot National Monument, the Hopi name for which, David said, was Johsahovi. The Bluebird Clan had lived here, always in the shadow of the Bear Clan, who at the time had inhabited what is now Montezuma Castle, another national monument. David explained that, as the prophecies commanded, one day the Bear Clan moved on their inevitable journey toward the mesas and the Bluebird Clan abandoned their village and followed. They had left a live infant in one of the

chief's houses. This was done, George said, so that the Bluebird Clan would always have the right to return.

At the trim little museum–reception center maintained by the Park Service, the old man marched up to an attendant and explained who he was and that his clan had originated there (information not given in the museum's literature). When he asked if the baby was still there, I expected the worst from the smug-looking guard. But no, the guard hesitated and said that actually the archaeologists had found the remains of an infant when they had excavated the place in the 1930s. It had been reinterred out of respect, he said.

In fact, several infants had been discovered in the ruin, the literature stated. George thanked the guard and headed for the ruin, which was much like Wupatki but smaller, sitting, like it, on a knoll overlooking a valley through which a small river pursued its serpentine course. He found the place where the baby had been reburied and stood there silently for a long time. Then he headed for the roof, via a stairway the Park Service had temporarily barred on account of an invasion of bees. When I questioned his disobeying the Park Service's sign, he paused on the stairs, looked back at me with a cheerful glint in his eyes, and said, "This is my place. It's all right for *me* to go anywhere here. Come on."

From the roof, George looked around at the valley below and said, "I've never been here before. This is a good place. It's too bad we had to leave here. Of course when the Bear Clan left to go north we had to follow them. It's too bad. Maybe we could come back here some day. Look at all that water."

The exhibits at Tuzigoot did not show the Hopi name for the place and made no reference to the Hopi. The time frame given was much the same as Wupatki's. Yet far to the north and east, at what is called Navajo National Monument by the Park Service, is a ruin called Betatakin and by the Hopi Kywestima. Located in a great red recessed cave above the canyon floor and consisting of multiple dwellings and kivas stacked miraculously upon one another and joined by rickety ladders, it is known to have been inhabited by ancestral Hopi, and so the exhibits—up on the top of the canyon—say. The Hopi regard such ruins, dotted here and there about the area, as deliberately built (and abandoned) monuments—testimony to their migrations.

There is a problem of timing here. George and other Hopi state explicitly that the village of Shungopavi was the first true Hopi village to be established in the area where the Hopi are concentrated. It was located down below the mesa among some rolling mounds of land that enjoyed a free-flowing spring (which can still be seen). Oraibi was the next Hopi village to be founded. It began because of a squabble that still engages the Hopi conscience. The Shungopavi chief's brother, said George, a young man named Machito, was told to plant his own sweet corn instead of relying on his brother's. Outraged, Machito disappeared from Shungopavi, and before long some men out on a rabbit hunt found him living in a cave on the side of the mesa where Oraibi is located.

The chief went to ask his brother to return, but Machito was adamant. His wife joined him, and they eventually moved up to the top of the mesa, accepting other newly arriving people into their village. George suggested a kind of inappropriateness about all these doings: it seems that the Oraibis allowed others to come into their village without first proving they had some talent or skill to contribute. Machito, George said, didn't want to have any religion in the village because "he didn't like staying up all night." Finally, he acceded to the need for religion and more or less reluctantly permitted the Oraibis to be taught religion by the Shungopavis.

People from Oraibi and the rest of Third Mesa grumble about this account. "Those people from Shungopavi," I've heard people complain, "think they're the beginning and the end." Be that as it may, it is generally conceded that Shungopavi was the first village to be established on the Hopi mesas and that the Bear Clan established it. So the Bear Clan left Montezuma Castle at some point in history and, followed by the Bluebird Clan, went to Wupatki. From there they journeyed to the Hopi mesas, and before long Oraibi was also established. But if Oraibi was established in the year 1150, then the Bear Clan would have to have left Wupatki earlier than the 1225 date given by the Park Service. There is a gap of about 100 years.

Is oral history more reliable than archaeology? Oral history changes—and at Hopi, depending on whom you're listening to, it differs. At the same time, given new finds, new interpretations, new refinements of dating methods, archaeological dates are often altered.

●

In 1980 the Hopi, along with the Indian peoples along the Rio Grande, celebrated the tricentennial of the Pueblo Revolt of 1680, when these people rose up as one and ran the Spanish out of the area. The Hopi portion of the celebration was a seminar at the newly erected Hopi Civic Center, in which experts on

Hopi from various universities explained their findings to a small but intent group of Hopi. Among the scholars was Fred Eggan, perhaps the most noted anthropologist of modern times to deal with Hopi. His fieldwork among the Hopi had spanned several decades, beginning before World War II.

Basing his hypothesis on linguistic, archaeological, and anthropological data, Dr. Eggan proposed the theory that the Hopi had long, long ago been among the large group of hunters and gatherers inhabiting the Great Basin, living in small familial bands, getting together socially perhaps once a year. In due course they had moved south and found canyons such as the Grand Canyon to their liking—safe places to live—and had dwelled there for a long time, finally emerging from the canyons to inhabit the Hopi mesas amidst various other

affection because of his basic friendliness and his devotion to Hopi ceremonies (he is an antelope priest).

"The Hopi people," Ferrell declared, "arrived through a place called Sipapuni via a reed, from the Underworld. At the time, we knew about corn already. We had come from the Third World to the Fourth. We did not come from the north only, or from the south. We came from the four directions, as our prophecies told us, and we arrived here. This was after a great deal of journeying and settling and moving. It was all long after we had emerged from Sipapuni with the knowledge of corn and other things."

Thus there were presented two apparently irreconcilable versions of Hopi origins—one from science and one from Hopi belief. Both views will be examined in greater detail, starting with the archaeological account.

People have been using the Hopi mesa area for at least 5,000 years and probably as long as ten thousand. Not much is known about the first 8,000 years, except that the people hunted locally available game and gathered wild plants; only toward the end of this period was maize (corn) introduced—no doubt from the south, in Mexico, where it first became domesticated. From A.D. 1 to about A.D. 700 a culture was developed in the Four Corners area by a group that archaeologists call the Basketmaker People. They lived in dry caves, rock shelters, also in villages of two to five pit houses, with superstructures of pole walls chinked with mud. By about A.D. 500 the people had learned to make pottery by baking clay, their pit houses were deeper and more elaborate, and village size grew. By about A.D. 700 beans and cotton were introduced, along with various architectural details borrowed from people to the north and to the south.

peoples. It may have been that while they lived in certain canyons, people from the south had introduced them to the planting and harvesting of corn and beans and they had become the agriculturalists they still are—to one degree or another. The language of the original people of the Great Basin was Shoshonean, and that is a branch of the Uto-Aztecan language group, into which the Hopi language taxonomically falls.

After Dr. Eggan's presentation, Ferrell Secakuku arose from the bleachers to speak. The owner of the Second Mesa trading post, Ferrell, though regarded by some with suspicion because of his success in business (he travels annually to Europe or China with his family), is generally held in great

At about this time the first substantial presence in the Hopi mesa area was established, a village on Antelope Mesa (east of what is now Keams Canyon), whose people appear to have farmed the valley below and used a local spring. This is the period that archaeologists call Pueblo I. Masonry walls came into use, rising above pit houses; soon pit houses were abandoned for above-ground dwellings. Some pit houses continued in use as ceremonial buildings. People were settling down to a more sedentary life. Fifty percent of their diet came from agriculture.

Between 900 and 1100 (the period called Pueblo II) there were many more masonry villages in the area, but they were smaller in size, with the houses ranged—much as they still are in Hopi villages—around a central plaza in which the underground kivas were built. The villages in the valleys were abandoned for settlements on the mesa-tops.

The next 200 years (Pueblo III) saw a drying of the climate, and farming became more risky. Most of the growing population of the Colorado Plateau clustered in larger villages—some of them containing up to hundreds of rooms—in the area of the Hopi mesas and also in the well-watered region of the Rio Grande, to the east. The villages of Oraibi and Awatovi were founded during this period, at the end of which there was a great drought lasting nearly twenty-five years, which archaeologists believe was the final straw in moving the people off most of the Colorado Plateau.

The drought caused changes on the Hopi mesas. Of forty-seven villages, thirty-six were abandoned. The eleven that remained, and three new ones that were soon established, were much larger than the older ones, and the popula-

tion of the mesas grew. The period that follows—Pueblo IV, from 1350 to 1540—is what archaeologists refer to as the ancestral Hopi period.

The larger villages called for greater social organization, and village chieftainships arose, along with the use of the kiva as a center for the sharing and redistribution of food in what may have been a time of stress. The houses—of stone cemented with adobe and then plastered inside—were virtually indistinguishable from the older houses of present-day Hopi, except that they were often multistoried. There were rooms for living in, rooms for storage, and special rooms for such activities as grinding corn. The kivas were rectangular and nearly identical to those of today. (To the east, kivas were round.) During this time, outcrops of subbituminous coal on Second Mesa and Antelope Mesa were mined, and the coal was used for heating homes and kivas and for making pottery. The Hopi were thus among the first people in the world to use coal for such purposes. (A Hopi friend told me that long ago it became obvious that the fumes from the coal were too noxious to allow in the houses and kivas, so a kachina arrived and told the people to use coal only for making pottery—outdoors.)

The Pueblo IV period saw a considerable revolution in the decoration of pottery. Yellow pottery replaced the white, gray, and red pottery of the past, perhaps because of the use of coal. The simple, repetitive designs that had been painted on the pottery—and also on the walls of some kivas, for about 500 years—were rather suddenly abandoned in favor of the dramatic asymmetrical, curvilinear designs that the Hopi now favor. This, archaeologists suggest, signaled some dramatic change in world view, and that may have been occasioned by the arrival of the kachina cult. Figures that are strongly reminiscent of kachinas begin to appear in the kiva murals of this period—at Hopi and at Zuni in the Rio Grande pueblos to the east. This religious society, it is speculated, came from the south: there is a petroglyph near El Paso with a similar figure that has been dated A.D. 1150.

Archaeologists surmise that the kachina cult was accepted so promptly because it represented another means of gaining control over a wayward environment still marked by the aftereffects of the great drought of 1276–1299. Also, the kachinas fit in with the growing sophistication of social stratification in which various chiefdoms for various purposes (such as defense or the timing of agricultural efforts) were arising and when an organized effort for redistributing food was of increasing importance.

By the 1500s Hopi culture was well established as a unity, not unlike its present status—a highly developed culture with an elaborate ritual cycle, a complex social organization, and a finely tuned agricultural system able to take advantage of the moisture trapped in the dunes that the southwesterly winds heap up against the mesas, of the occasional flooding of the washes (altogether dry for most of the year), of the flow of moisture out of the ends of arroyos, and, in a few areas, able to irrigate from springs.

•

On a July morning in 1540, there must have been considerable consternation in the villages along the eastern escarpment of Antelope Mesa. For in the valley below they saw an encampment unlike anything they had ever seen. There were men with metal body parts. There were strange-looking four-legged beasts,

much larger than antelopes, and some of these were part animal and part metal-chested man. They could see the man part separate itself from the animal and walk around, and they must have wondered what was happening to their world. One thing they could not have known was that they had passed out of prehistory into history.

A thin column of Spanish soldiers had snaked its way from the south, from what is now Mexico, responding to tales of enormous wealth—of the Seven Cities of Gold lying supine and to be had for the taking in the north. Led by Coronado, the Spanish soldiers had been thoroughly discouraged when they encountered what seemed to them the squalid and poor villages of the Zuni, and the similar pueblos (as they called them) of the Rio Grande. In due course they heard about some fabled cities to the northwest, probably from Zuni people with whom the Hopi periodically traded or warred. It is possible to speculate that perhaps the Zuni thought they could rid themselves of the Spanish by tempting them to go to Hopi. In any event, Coronado dispatched Pedro de Tobar and the Franciscan friar Juan de Padilla with a small band of soldiers and Zuni guides to seek out the gold-encrusted Hopi civilization.

When they arrived at Antelope Mesa, men came down armed with bows and shields and wooden clubs, and drew lines on the ground which they evidently were forbidding the newcomers to cross. An attempt at communication was made…a horse lurched, as if to cross the line, and was hit in the cheek with a Hopi club. The friar complained about wasting time, the soldiers yelled a battle cry and, according to a Spanish account, "ran down" many of the Indians, driving the rest up the mesa. Later the Spanish established a

camp below the mesa and the Hopi returned, seeking peace and bringing gifts of cotton and corn and birds and pine nuts. They gave the Spanish some turquoises, "but not many," wrote the ungrateful chronicler. Disgusted at not having found gold, Tobar and his men promptly returned to Coronado at Zuni.

At best, as far as the Spanish were concerned, the Hopi represented a rather remote outpost of savage souls to be saved for the Church. The Spanish called these people *Moqui*—a name (probably derived from the Zuni) that stuck into the twentieth century, somewhat to the dismay of the Hopi themselves, since, in their language, the word means "dies," or "is dying." Thus did the Hopi enter what we call history.

●

As we have seen, archaeology's version of Hopi origins and migrations differs greatly from the Hopi version recorded in their oral history. The following account gives the general outline, and some of the many variations in detail, of the Hopi version.

In the beginning there was endless space, in which nothing existed but Tawa the sun spirit, who contrived to gather some of the elements of space and inject some of his own substance into them and thereby create the First World, inhabited largely by insect-like creatures which lived in dark caves and fought among themselves. Dissatisfied, Tawa sent a new spirit, Spider Grandmother, down to prepare them for a long trip. She led them on a long journey during which they changed form, grew fur on their bodies, acquired tails, and took on the shapes of dogs and wolves and bears. They arrived in the Second World, but still Tawa

was displeased, for these creatures did not understand the meaning of life any more than their predecessors had. So Spider Grandmother was dispatched again, and while she led them on their second journey Tawa created a Third World, lighter and moist. By the time they arrived in the Third World they had become people. Spider Grandmother cautioned them to renounce evil and live in harmony.

They built villages and planted corn. But it was cold. Again Spider Grandmother arrived; she taught them to weave and to make pots. But the pots could not be baked and the corn did not grow well because of the chill. One day a hummingbird arrived, explaining that he had been sent by Masauwu, who lived in yet another world above the sky called the Upper World and was the owner of fire and the caretaker of the place of the dead. The hummingbird taught the people to make fire with a drill and left.

They learned to bake their pottery so that it wouldn't break; they warmed their fields by lighting fires; they cooked their meat instead of eating it raw. Things were better in the Third World now.

But soon sorcerers (*powakus*) began to unleash evil in the world, making medicines that would harm people and turn their minds from virtue. Men gambled instead of tending their fields. Women revolted. Rains failed to come, and the corn failed.

One account says that Spider Grandmother came once again, to warn them, telling the people who still had good hearts that they should leave this world and go to the Upper World. Another account says that a chief and his wise men prayed for four days and made prayer feathers and then asked the mockingbird

(*yaapa*) to help them. He said that they should first ask the canary, who agreed, so the two birds set out to help, singing (by now, they had changed into two handsome men) and calling for the eagle. The eagle, they hoped, would fly up until he found an opening in the sky. He tried and failed. The hawk was summoned and he tried too, returning nearly dead from exhaustion but certain that there was an opening. Next the swallow was asked to go, and he nearly reached the opening but was badly buffeted by the winds and returned.

Lastly, the shrike was asked to help. Noting the three previous failures, he sought assurances that all the people assembled had pure hearts. Reassured, he flew off and he not only discovered the opening but flew up into it (finding it to be much like the people's kiva) and out the other side, where there was a brighter, better world but one devoid of people. The shrike returned with the news.

Elated, the Hopi resolved to go to this other world, but the question remained: how to get there? By some accounts Spider Grandmother, and by others a boy, reminded the people of the chipmunk, who lived on pine nuts and might help them plant a tall tree. His aid enlisted, the chipmunk planted a spruce and, with the proper prayers, made it grow, but not high enough to reach the sky. He then planted a "fir-pine," which grew only slightly higher. A "long-needle" pine also failed. The chipmunk asked if someone with an evil heart was present, and all the people there assured him of their pure intentions. The fourth time, a bamboo was tried, and the chipmunk ran up the stalk four times to tug it upward. Finally, exhausted, he asked the four birds to fly up and see if it had grown high enough. Only the shrike made it to the top, and he sat on an uppermost branch as the plant grew through the opening. This opening was the

FAR LEFT: Father and Mother Corn, perfect ears of corn surrounded with herbs, to be placed in the roasting pit of sweet corn.

NEAR LEFT: Abbott Sekaquaptewa working in a field at his family ranch.

BELOW: A young prairie falcon is taken to a new home and family in Shipaulovi. The Hopi classify all falcons and hawks as eagles.

Sipapuni. Then he returned with the good news. The chipmunk explained that the people could climb up inside the bamboo reed, since it was hollow.

The chief sent forth priests to draw lines of cornmeal; any evil person who crossed the lines to try to reach the bamboo would perish. The One Horn priests went north and west to draw the lines; the Two Horn priests went south and east—this was the origin of those two religious societies. In due course and after the proper prayers and preparations, the people of good heart made it up through the great bamboo reed and reached the Upper World—the Fourth World of the Hopi.

An untoward event occurred almost immediately: a young girl died. The chief suspected that a witch might have managed to come up the bamboo with them and, after some inquiry, another girl confessed. The people were about to hurl her back into the world below, but she protested that anyone who died in the Fourth World would return to the Underworld (the Third World) and be safe. She proved this, showing them the dead girl, now back in the Underworld and playing happily, so the people permitted the witch girl to remain, realizing that she had already contaminated the Fourth World and that good and evil are always present, always at odds.

Most things at Hopi are done in fours. On the fourth day, they noticed a distant fire and the next morning some young men started out to see who might have lit the fire. They found only some gigantic human footprints. The chief decided to send four men out, with a plaque filled with prayer feathers, to find whoever had left the footprints. Eventually they reached the fire and found a huge man hunched over the embers. They called to him three times, but he would not

look at them. On their fourth try, he said he was surprised to see them, for no one had ever come so close to him. As he spoke he turned, and the men were confronted with a terrible mask behind which was an awful, bloody face. The huge masked man accepted the prayer feathers with pleasure and explained that he was Masauwu, the god of the Upper World, and was therefore their god now. Since he also was the god of the dead, he explained, anyone who died would come to him and he would see to it that the dead person made it safely back to the Underworld. Ever since, Masauwu has been worshiped by the Hopi.

There was a great deal of work to be done to make the Upper World habitable, it seems, and by one account much of this was accomplished by Spider Grandmother and her two grandsons, the twin boy warriors Pokanghoya and Polongahoya. Buckskin discs were hurled into the sky to create the moon and the sun, providing light and warmth. The landscape was all of a sameness and very muddy. The twins, playing a kind of field hockey, raced about the land, and wherever their feet touched, it grew firm; they heaped up mud and this became mountains. They created Tokonavi (Navajo Mountain) and Neuvatikao (San Francisco Peaks) and Muyovi (the Rio Grande). Trees and grass came into being wherever they passed.

Meanwhile the mockingbird, at the request of the chief, sorted the people out, this one to be a Hopi and speak the Hopi language, that one to be a Navajo and speak the Navajo language, and so on, until there were Ute, Apache, Comanche, Supai, Pima, Zuni, and the white men.

Then the mockingbird placed several ears of corn on the ground—each of a different color—and explained that each ear carried with it a destiny. For example, the yellow corn would bring a full life but a short one, while the short blue corn would bring an arduous life but a long one. The leader of the Navajo quickly reached for the yellow ear of corn, and then all the others made their choices, until there was only the blue ear of corn left. As the Hopi leader picked it up, he told his people that it would bring them a difficult life with much adversity, but that the Hopi would survive all adversities, whereas other tribes would one day perish.

The next day the people left in the directions the mockingbird had assigned them. The last to go were the white men and the Hopi—and the witch girl (the powaku). The leader of the pahanas said that since the witch girl had great knowledge, she could join them. With that, they left, heading south, and the Hopi leader warned his people that the pahanas would learn evil as well as good, so the people should listen very cautiously if they encountered white people. But one day a particular pahana would come and bring harmony and kindness and peace.

Spider Grandmother then instructed the Hopi to be mindful of their gods—Tawa the sun spirit; Masauwu; Muyingwa, the spirit of germination; Balolokong, the water serpent, who brings rain and is in charge of springs.

The Hopi then left, heading east, knowing that when they arrived in the place they were destined to reach, the place they would stay, they would know it by the appearance of a great star. They split into bands, ultimately going in various directions, and these bands became the Hopi clans.

One band, on its journey east from what is now the Little Colorado River, came across a dead bear and decided they would call themselves the Bear Clan.

Another band found the same bear, took some of its skin and made straps to help in carrying their heavy loads, and became the Bear Strap Clan. The next band to pass found the bear little more than a skeleton; bluebirds were perched on it, and they became the Bluebird Clan. The fourth band, finding a spider in its web on the skeleton, became the Spider Clan. A fifth band, having seen a gopher near the bear's skeleton, became the Gopher Clan. Finally, long afterward, another band happened by; finding a strange greasy substance in one of the bear's eye sockets, they became the Greasy Eye Cavity Clan.

Eventually the Bear Clan encountered Masauwu and asked him to be their leader. He refused, saying that they should choose their leader from among themselves. But he offered them the use of certain lands down below the mesa, and eventually they arrived there and built the village called Shungopavi; the other associated clans arrived in due course and were assigned lands and roles by the Bear Clan. Other groups drifted in over time—the Parrot Clan from the south, who were then asked to give up some of their land for the Sun Forehead Clan, who were the warriors, assigned to guard the perimeters, and finally the Sun Clan.

Meanwhile the Snake Clan had migrated from Tokonavi to the Walpi area, bringing with them the wonderful power to bring rain, learned from the snakes. They were eventually joined there by the Water Clan from the south, who also had wonderful powers to bring rain and make springs.

Thus did the clans gather from the four directions. As they migrated here and there, they left marks etched in the flat surfaces of rocks—often spirals or concentric rings—notifications to posterity that they had passed through on their way to the mesas.

LEFT: Valjean Joshvema surveys Hopi lands from a high promontory at Kachina Points, west of the Hopi mesas.

The artist Milland Lomakema told us of one such petroglyph. It consists of a square with two wavy lines descending from the bottom corners. The Navajo, he said, claim it as their mark and interpret it to mean that they had always been traveling until they finally settled into this area. But Milland's father, a member of the Bear Strap Clan, says it is a memorial, or shrine, of his clan: the square represents what is now the Four Corners area and the two wavy lines represent the sides of the Grand Canyon valley, which leads to the Four Corners area. This is the route his clan is never to forget, a place that will always be wet and cannot ever be erased. Milland said his father goes each year to visit this shrine.

In the course of time, the clans made their way to Hopi mesa country, each bringing some special talent or ceremony that would help all the people. Hopi history is full of accounts of villages being started, encountering various kinds of difficulties, and breaking up to form other villages. For example, far to the south the Water Clan at one time established the village of Palatkwapi, to which other clans came, such as the Eagle Clan, the Sand Clan, the Tobacco Clan, and the Rabbit Brush Clan. Before long, they forgot that according to their prophecies they were supposed to move on, and many began to forsake the old ways and truths. Evil entered the village, and the leaders pondered what they should do. Eventually the chief sacrificed one of his nephews, and on the fourth day after the boy's death a tremendous earthquake shook the village and, together with flooding rains, destroyed it. The great water serpent Balolokong appeared from the water. Two children were sent into the flood, carrying prayer offerings, and the fearsome-looking serpent, instead of devouring them, instructed them in the ways of water. The children returned to their people with the secrets of

the Water Clan. The various clans that were assembled above the destroyed village split up and moved on, to found other villages here and there before ultimately arriving in their present homes on the Hopi mesas.

•

In the year 1054, Chinese astronomers observed a tremendous star that suddenly appeared, shining for several months so brightly that it could be seen during the day. This we now know was a supernova, the explosion of a star in its death throes. There are petroglyphs in the American West and in South America which strongly suggest that some people living in this hemisphere saw and took note of this extraordinary star. I have known at least one Hopi to speculate that perhaps that was the star that told the first arriving Hopi bands that they had finally reached the place where they should permanently settle. It is unlikely that anyone will ever know.

In the Hopi narrative of the gathering of the clans is to be found the meaning of the hundreds of ruins seen throughout northern Arizona, ruins that are called by historians and archaeologists *Anasazi*—a Navajo word that ironically means "ancestors of the enemy." These ruins are places where the Navajo fear to go but where Hopi still go to commune with the spirits of their ancestors.

And then, none too auspiciously, it must have seemed, the pahanas arrived from the east. The next four and a half centuries were to be a long saga of remarkably passive resistance, given the circumstances, to continuing efforts to deny Hopi society its religion and its land. It is estimated that only some 5 percent of all Hopi are Christians; they live in essentially the same place they have lived in for a millennium—probably the most culturally intact group of native

The element of remoteness cannot be overestimated. As late as the 1830s there was a legend among the mountain men who were opening the path between Santa Fe and California, and who had passed through Hopi country, that there was a group of short Welsh people, long gone from Wales and living in the high country near the Colorado River, who were so peaceful that when strangers came they hid in caves and pulled stones in after them, staying there until the strangers went away.

In 1540, after the Spanish left (having apparently done more damage than running down a few Hopi—in fact having demolished part of the village of Kwakiaka north of Awatovi on Antelope Mesa) the Hopi no doubt recalled their chief's warning long ago to regard the white man with caution; indeed, some forty years later, in 1583, Kwakiaka and a nearby village, Sikyatki, had been abandoned when another Spaniard, Antonio de Espeja, led a few soldiers and Zuni to Hopi and persuaded them to help him find mines. In the 1590s, when Juan de Oñate established the province of Nuevo México and set up his headquarters at the San Juan pueblo on the Rio Grande, he included the Hopi territory in his province and soon heard rumors that the Hopi were ready to submit to the rule of the King of Spain. But it was to be thirty years before a missionary would visit the Hopi mesas. Beginning in 1629, missionaries began to arrive, and the Hopi cooperated, building missions for the friars in Awatovi, Shungopavi, and Oraibi. A friar wrote in 1630 that 10,000 Hopi had been converted—no doubt an outrageous exaggeration, there hardly ever having been so many Hopi living at one time.

people on the continent. Much of this is due to their isolation in the remote high plains and mesas, far off the beaten track as the West began to be explored. And some of the isolation, in the earlier periods, had to do with the obstacles put in the way of travelers by the dangerous and warlike Ute and Apache, who roamed the area between the Hopi mesas and the Rio Grande. Much also must have been the result of the shrewdness and determination of the Hopi people themselves. And in part the isolation no doubt had to do with the facts that the Spanish empire was suffering from an extreme case of dry rot even as its first expeditions were leaving Mexico to explore the north country, that the brief tenure by the Mexicans in North America was an unmitigated failure, and that until the beginning of the twentieth century the Anglos had too many other fish to fry to bother much with the Hopi.

The fact that few if any soldiers accompanied the missionaries in the ensuing fifty years does suggest that the Hopi acquiesced in the friars' hegemony in their lives. One incident suggests otherwise: caught in an act of idolatry, a Hopi named Juan Cuna was whipped in public, then hauled into the church and beaten again. Unsatisfied, the friar then poured turpentine on Cuna and set him on fire. The Hopi protested his death, and the friar was subsequently convicted of that and other crimes and reassigned to New Mexico. It is also likely that the Hopi may have pretended to accept the Spanish religion, meanwhile practicing their own in secret. A leader of the Wuwutsim society told me that the friars had sought to ban the Hopi ceremonies at Oraibi, so the Oraibis simply took their ceremonial materials off to Kachina Points, an awesome outcrop of red mesas and knife-edged ridges some miles to the west, and would go there to carry out their ceremonies.

On the other hand, in 1650, when the people of Taos asked the Hopi to join in a rebellion against the Spanish, the Hopi declined. Despite certain instances of Castilian brutality, there must have been a kind of modus vivendi for half a century.

Not elsewhere, however. Continuing suppression of the religion of the Pueblos along the Rio Grande soon led to a great humiliation of the Spanish in their effort to conquer the Western Hemisphere for the King and the Church. Led by a San Juan priest named Po-peh and by other leaders from the pueblos strung north and south along the river, the Pueblo people rose up as one on the morning of August 10, 1680, and slaughtered Franciscan missionaries, Spanish ranchers, and soldiers, led a siege of Santa Fe that lasted for several days, and ended by forcing the governor and a thousand refugees to march painfully and arduously out of New Mexico to El Paso.

The Hopi joined in this revolt (indeed one Hopi historian suggests that it was a Bear Clan man from Oraibi who was the actual instigator). In any event, the Hopi turned on the missionaries in their villages and, so far as is known, killed them all.

Promptly, fearing a return of the Spanish in force, the Hopi moved three of their villages up off the desert floor, establishing the village of Walpi on the narrow knife-edged tip of First Mesa, moving Shungopavi and Mishongnovi up onto Second Mesa and, historians say, soon establishing Shipaulovi high up on an even more inaccessible part of Second Mesa, where ceremonial paraphernalia could be stored to keep them out of Spanish hands.

Twelve years after the rebellion, Diego de Vargas led the Spanish back into New Mexico, where the Rio Grande Pueblos were in social chaos. Hundreds of the people from the east had fled, many coming to Hopi, where they were accepted. A group of Tewa-speaking people arrived and sought refuge. The village of Hano was established for them near Walpi on First Mesa (it remains a Tewa-speaking village), and Payupki was established north of the other Second Mesa villages, becoming a melting pot of Rio Grande people. Vargas soon came to Hopi, found the people ready to resist, and offered not to attack them if they would swear allegiance.

The people agreed, and Vargas left. More people from the east arrived as the Spanish reconquest of the Rio Grande progressed, and some people, apparently at Awatovi, observing the success of the reconquest, sent a mission to the Spanish, offering to rebuild the churches and asking that priests be sent to them.

Before long there was a severe split at Awatovi between those who had welcomed the Franciscans and those who wished to follow the old ways. Accounts vary in detail, but apparently the village chief became so distressed by the Christianizing of people of his village and what he perceived as the resulting corruption of Hopi values that he ventured to enlist the aid of the other villages to exterminate the Christians. People from Shungopavi, Walpi, and Oraibi agreed, and one night they swept down on Awatovi, trapping the Christians, killing all the Christianized men, and sacking the village. The women and children were led away and divided up among the other villages; Awatovi clan lands were distributed among the villages as well—Oraibi for some reason getting none. Awatovi was allowed to crumble into a ruin, and Hopi habitation on Antelope Mesa was essentially at an end. The ruin can still be visited (with a Hopi guide), but many Hopi prefer not to go there.

A Hopi told me that some members of the Tobacco Clan in Awatovi were warned the night of the attack and left town, saying they were going on a rabbit hunt. The next morning, several miles to the east, they turned to see the village on fire, and they continued east to ancestral lands in Canyon de Chelly. They lived there for a while, planting the peach trees that are still growing there, intermarried with Navajo, and eventually returned to live below Antelope Mesa. After more interbreeding with Navajo, they moved farther west and south; now, speaking Navajo and living as Navajo, they remain members of the Tobacco Clan, being descended from two Hopi women.

After the destruction of Awatovi, the Spanish made a few half-hearted efforts to punish the Hopi but they failed. High in their village fortresses, the Hopi were

largely impregnable to an ever-weakening Spanish presence. A large number of the Rio Grande people were persuaded to return, and the village of Payupki was eventually abandoned. But this was, to all intents and purposes, the end of Spanish influence among the Hopi people, who, in the words of one historian, were probably "the most famous 'apostates' in the history of Spanish Christianity."

After a century of contact, the people of the mesas had taken what they found useful from the Spanish—sheep, burros, metal, various fruits and vegetables—but had given up little. Indeed, they had, after Awatovi, achieved an unprecedented unity among the various villages—if only a unified determination to remain free of Spanish dominion. And of course the Hopi had moved to the mesa-tops out of fear of the Spanish.

Another reason that moving the villages up on the mesas had seemed prudent was that from about the early 1600s on, raids from Ute and Apache had been increasingly common. By the early 1800s these warlike nomads had virtually cut the Hopi and Zuni off from any contact with the east. A brief Mexican regime had almost no contact with the Hopi, and the marauding nomads went almost completely unchecked, particularly harassing the eastern Pueblos but causing increasing pain to those to the west. The life of Hopi went on as it had for centuries, the ceremonial cycle intact and its twin, the agricultural cycle, generally prosperous. Other white men, Anglos, began to show up now and then—indeed some mountain men had made their brief and largely harmless appearances even before the Mexicans were ejected from the American Southwest by the Treaty of Guadalupe de Hidalgo in 1848. The main scourge that the Hopi faced, besides the nomadic raiders, was another cultural heritage brought by the pahana—

smallpox. Periodically the population of the mesas was savagely reduced from thousands to hundreds by this scourge, and one can only imagine the horror, the fear, the recriminations, the accusations of witchcraft and evil-heartedness, the pleas to the gods that must have accompanied these catastrophes.

During the 1850s and 1860s the visits of the whites were more frequent; often they were government officials seeking to gain information in order to aid the Hopi in their frequent experiences of Navajo encroachment. These contacts were civil and polite, and in some parts of Hopi it became possible for people to think that these Anglos might represent the true pahana who was to return to the aid of Hopi. Yet other whites began to arrive from the north—these were the Mormons. A significant attempt was made by Mormon missionaries not only to convert the Hopi but to persuade them to move to Utah. The conversion attempts failed, by and large, though a few Hopi did move away.

There is still an organized Mormon effort at Hopi and there are still a handful of Mormonized Hopi. No one should set himself or herself up to deny the right of missionaries to proselytize—to do so is to deny a basic American pattern of salesmanship of ideas as well as material objects. But it is hard to pass by this topic without mentioning that for years the Mormons read their sacred texts as saying that dark-skinned people who took on the Mormon faith would eventually find their skin getting lighter—since one of the attributes of Mormonism was to be white. I spent an embarrassing ride in a pickup truck once with two Mormonized Hopi women who had convinced themselves that their skin had become lighter. The Mormon fathers have reinterpreted their scripture, and "pure" has replaced "white." The few Hopi

who are Mormon no longer have to watch their skin anxiously for signs of progress.

Nevertheless by the 1870s there was a sizable Mormon establishment in the area of Moenkopi, northwest of the Hopi mesas, and by this time the Santa Fe railroad had pushed westward, some seventy miles south of the mesas, through Winslow. Apparently these two impending impacts—as well as the growing problem of Navajo encroachment on what the Hopi believed to be their land— led to the signing of the executive order by President Arthur in 1882 establishing a rectangle of some 2,400,000 acres to be set aside for the use of the "Moqui and other such Indians as the Secretary of the Interior may see fit to settle thereon." This phrasing turned out to be the weasel words that have dogged the Hopi for a century and muddied the increasingly unhappy relations between the Hopi and the Navajo.

With the establishment of the Hopi Reservation, the presence of the U.S. government increased. A series of Indian agents trekked into Hopi and unwittingly, over the years, persuaded the Hopi that the true pahana was yet to arrive. The first agent, James Gallaher, arrived in Keams Canyon to establish his official residency in May 1887. One of his tasks was to build a school, in response to a plea from twenty Hopi, including the leaders of Walpi and Shungopavi. Some Hopi wanted the white man's school; others did not. A new kind of schism was beginning to open up among the Hopi.

The agents who served over the years had largely dictatorial powers and rarely much understanding or affection for the Hopi in their charge. Based on the belief that Hopi ceremonies were pagan and inappropriate, the federal policy was not only to attempt to get all Hopi children away from their homes to the white man's school, but also to pressure them to convert to Christianity and forswear their traditional religion and ceremonies. The agents handed out land to various missionaries, invariably interfering with ancient Hopi beliefs about ownership of land and thus causing friction. Further friction developed when Hopi parents found out that their children could not go to school on Sunday and the Christian holidays but had to go to school on the days of Hopi ceremonies. The Oraibis were soon virtually in full revolt, refusing to send their children to the school. The agent in Keams Canyon, then known officially as the School Superintendent, called in the troops from Fort Defiance in New Mexico on December 28, 1890, and twenty-eight soldiers forcibly rounded up 104 children and hauled them off to school.

In 1891 the policy of land allotment was inaugurated. The procedure was to offer individual Hopi parcels of land below the mesas, which they would own the way a person from a white culture owns a piece of real estate. Hopi were offered free lumber for building homes if they agreed to take on the ownership of pieces of land carved out of the map by the agents. Traditionally, no Hopi owns land. All the land around the mesas, for virtually as far as the eye can see, is clan land—originally handed out by the Bear Clan to other clans and, within the clan system, parceled out to individuals for their use. The dispute over the housing below Shipaulovi with which this book began was essentially a dispute over clan rights to the land. The clans are in frequent conflict over such matters, but to offer our white culture's notion of ownership of land, with all the exclusivity and individualized authority that it

implies, was a brilliant and subtle attack on the basic fabric of Hopi culture. Fortunately, there were few takers.

In the next few years, day schools were opened in several of the villages, with many children staying away. By 1894 the allotment program had been largely abandoned. Only a handful of Hopi had taken the government up on its offer, and many had sought to halt the needed land surveys by hauling up the surveyors' stakes as soon as they were emplaced. Yet the "divide and conquer" tactic had had its effect. By the mid-1890s a schism was fully developed within Oraibi. The people who wished to go along with some government programs, particularly the schools, were called "friendlies," those opposed, "hostiles." The friendlies apparently perceived value in some of the new ways of the whites, or at least saw the need to cooperate with so evidently powerful a new presence. Hostiles began taking fields away from friendlies, and nineteen leaders of the hostiles were therefore rounded up and sent to Alcatraz for seven months. The last outbreak of smallpox, beginning in 1897, led to an enforced vaccination program that, since it was carried out with little attempt to educate the Hopi about its purpose, led to deeper suspicion on the part of many Hopi and widened the rift between the hostiles and the friendlies. This polarization has persisted into recent times, with the label "progressives" replacing "friendlies" and "traditionalists" replacing "hostiles."

The appointment of Charles E. Burton as Agent to the Moqui Reservation in 1900 furthered the basic policy of trying to eliminate the Hopi way of life. Among his determinations was that any Hopi man or boy who refused to have his hair cut would have it cut by force. A considerable amount of force was, in fact, employed, and in 1903, a young white schoolteacher, a woman, appalled by this treatment of the Hopi, resigned and became the leader of an attempt to gain nationwide publicity and sympathy for the Hopi. White scientists, writers, artists, and photographers, who had become more frequent visitors to the Hopi mesas (and were regarded with justified suspicion by the agents in Keams Canyon), joined the crusade. The ensuing uproar led finally to the reversal of the hair-cutting dictum and the firing of a couple of federal employees, but Burton remained on the job.

National monuments Tuzigoot (*left*), Wupatki, and other ruins in the surrounding area were villages left behind when the Hopi clans migrated to their present mesas.

Meanwhile forces were at work among the Hopi. The most significant eruption in modern times of the volcano that is Hopi society was about to take place: Oraibi, the moral center and the largest of the Hopi villages, housing about half of the 2,000 Hopi on the reservation, was about to split into four.

One can trace the causes of this eruption back to the 1830s, when a benighted band of Anglo mountain men, for no more valid reason than the insouciant feeling of being part of a new nation's manifest destiny, opened fire on some Hopi men tending their fields and killed several of them. The victims happened to be from Oraibi, and there arose among the Oraibis, not at all unreasonably, a belief that the new breed of white man was probably not the long-awaited pahana. But the seeds of this event may go back much further, perhaps back to the original Hopi prophecies that led the people to the mesas and foretold the altercation by which Oraibi originally came into being. In any event, the chiefs of Oraibi, from the 1830s on, were extremely suspicious of the white man, and many, though not all, Oraibis shared this feeling.

In the 1880s, when the U.S. government began to impose its presence on the mesas, the chief of Oraibi was a man named Lololoma. Along with a number of other Hopi leaders, he was invited to Washington through the intercession of the trader Keams (after whom Keams Canyon was named). Upon his return, he could explain that the people in Washington wanted the Hopi to move down from the mesas, the better to avoid Navajo depredations—a thought that must have seemed passing strange to the Hopi, and a thought, the leaders reported, they had rejected out of hand. But Lololoma had seen so many wonderful things in the East that he had changed his mind. The future lay with the acceptance of the white man's ways. This caused many Oraibis to flock to the banner of Lomahongyoma, a member of the Warrior society and of the Spider Clan. Lololoma belonged, of course, to the Bear Clan, and the two clans had acquired their names in association with the same bear corpse. They were, in this way, brothers.

By the turn of the century both men had passed on their chieftainships, and their points of view, to new chiefs. By 1889, the hostiles built a new kiva in Oraibi, where they would practice the important ceremonies, such as initiations and the Soyal, at the same time as those ceremonies were practiced by the friendlies. This was, of course, appalling, since harmony was essential to the success of the ceremonies. The centrality of leadership had been riven, the religious societies broken in two—certain catastrophe. Historian Harry C. James wrote that "Tewaquaptewa [now the leader of the friendlies] frequently expressed an almost oriental sense of destiny as the reason for proceeding as he felt obligated to do."

In 1904 some thirty people from Shungopavi joined the hostiles in Oraibi—a dissident group, it is said, invited by the hostiles in order to swell their ranks. Yet one can wonder if these Shungopavis had not come on their own, driven by their particular view of their responsibilities for Hopi propriety, to see to it that events took place in the manner already determined by the prophecies.

In 1906 there was a great deal of controversy over the twin ceremony of Niman, the Home Dance, performed in two antithetical kivas. The leader of the friendlies was persuaded by his advisors to throw the Shungopavis out before the Snake Dance, when a lot of white people would be present and might see the untoward results of the schism. He sent away to Moenkopi, considered a

Helen Sekaquaptewa signs a copy of her memoir, *Me and Mine*. As a child in the early 1900s, she was forcibly removed from her family in Oraibi and sent to the "white man's school" in Keams Canyon.

colony of Oraibi, and a large number of people from Moenkopi arrived to counter the weight of the Shungopavi people. There were scuffles and taunts from both sides and on September 8 there was a total confrontation, the two sides drawn up facing each other in great numbers. Finally the leader of the hostiles drew a line on the ground and stepped across it, toward Oraibi, challenging the friendlies to push him back over the line. If they couldn't, they would have to leave Oraibi forever—and vice versa. There ensued a shoving match during which the hostiles' leader was pushed straight up and then back over the line away from Oraibi.

The battle was over. The hostiles were required to leave the village at once, taking with them whatever they could carry. According to a previous plan, they were to journey back to Kywestima, the long-since-abandoned stopping-off place for certain of the clans as they had gathered—deep in the canyon of what is today known as Navajo National Monument. They never made it that far. About eight miles north of Oraibi, I have been told, they paused while a woman had a baby, and there they remained, founding the village of Hotevilla. Soldiers went on to Hotevilla; arrested the hostiles' leader, and put him in the Keams Canyon jail, a place he would inhabit often over the next two decades. The Shungopavis were rounded up and sent back to their village. The leaders of the friendlies were sent to the Sherman Institute in Riverside, California, to learn English, thus being deprived of the fruits of their victory.

Meanwhile at Hotevilla a winter had to be faced without homes or adequate food or clothing. The hostiles' leader, returning from jail, found himself not only with the problem of survival but also with another quarrel on his hands. Others of his group had begun to think the sensible path was a rapprochement with the people at Oraibi, and late that same year they led a contingent back to Oraibi. There they encountered continuing opposition, and they left in the fall of 1907, founding a new village, called Bacabi, a mile southeast of Hotevilla.

In 1910, the leader of the friendlies, Tewaquaptewa, returned to Oraibi, feeling betrayed by the white government that had exiled him to Riverside, and with a radically changed attitude. He began to encourage the friendlies to hostility, and in fact he finally turned against them, believing that Oraibi and its traditions would and should die out with him. Those remaining in the village who intended to become, or had become, Christians were ordered to leave, and they founded Kykotsmovi, at first called New Oraibi, below the mesa—now one of the largest Hopi villages and the seat of the Hopi Tribal Council. Tewaquaptewa left his succession in some disarray—a situation that began in the early 1940s, when he relinquished his position as kikmongwi, and remained controversial until the late 1970s, when his adopted son, Stanley, returned from California to take up the post. Where Oraibi used to be, resplendent in its teeming, many-storied greatness, stand the lightning-blasted remains of a Mennonite church (another failure) and a tattered group of buildings inhabited by a few families—an imminent ruin presided over by bitter elders still feeding on the old antagonisms, brooding from the mesa-top. There are new houses being built, but they are closer to the highway, some of them even across the highway, as if the people were trying to put some distance between them and the bad politics of the great Hopi village of old.

In 1929 the old leader of the hostiles died, also leaving his succession up in the air, where it remains. It is a common joke—on the other mesas—that anyone going to Hotevilla to pay respects to the kikmongwi will nave to stop off in four or five places. The largest of the Hopi villages in population, Hotevilla is a stronghold of the traditionalists, and considerably factionalized. A new village is planned, to the northwest, on Howell Mesa, to be peopled largely by Hopi from present-day Hotevilla. It will be a secular village, where ceremonies will not be performed.

Oraibi was scrambled like so many eggs.

Indeed, throughout Third Mesa, now split into four villages, where the major center of Oraibi once held single sway, some old ceremonies are dying out, as has been noted, and there are revivals of others. But since the 1930s no men have been initiated into the religious societies, we are told. Why is this? Certainly a group of people who for so many centuries had withstood the far more brutal, if not so clever, attempts of the Spanish to destroy their old ways could have withstood the "divide and conquer" strategy of so recent an arrival as the U.S. government.

Much is written about how both factions in the Oraibi split were careful to inform each other that bloody violence would not be needed. Yet, as we have seen, the Hopi have not been averse to such violence among themselves if it seemed necessary to maintain something of value. Awatovi was more than decimated in the early 1700s. It is suggested here and there that the splitting up of Oraibi was an event that had been prophesied long ago and that the prophecy had been held onto darkly and grimly throughout the centuries and finally acted out—as in the curiously ritualized confrontation in the fall of 1906, a harmless pushing match. And part of the prophecy, it has been said, was that not only would Oraibi split but also, at the same time, the Hopi religion would begin to come to an end.

Other explanations abound—that is, additional explanations. Peter Whitely, of the University of New Mexico's graduate school in anthropology, working in Bacabi, found indications that there may have been a class war worked out well in advance by the more aristocratic clans and societies to rid the village of lesser people. A Hopi suggested to me that it was a matter of freedom of religion, that the religious societies had become so tyrannical that a split was forced in an attempt to break the grip of religious intolerance and ecclesiastic iron rule. Rituals and the rigors of Hopi justice had perhaps become too elaborate and needed to be simplified. It is hard not to believe there was a well-worked-out script.

More than likely, the split was a result of all these causes and many more we shall never know, all interlayered and interwoven—an inextricably complex event in which the U.S. government and its nearly extraneous policies about hair styles and school attendance played the useful role of unwitting goat.

Nevertheless, school attendance continued to be an issue, as did the federal policy of eliminating the Hopi ceremonies. Agent after agent did his best to discourage the Hopi religion. There was one exception: Abraham Lawshe, who was superintendent during the year 1910. Not only did he suggest that stopping the Hopi ceremonies was the same as trying to stem the flow of Niagara; he also discredited the policy of allotting lands to individuals (which had periodically been revived), alluding to the policy's true purpose when he suggested in a report to Washington that no white man would ever find the land left over after such a program useful.

Lawshe was succeeded by Leo Crane, a despotic individual whose attitude toward the Hopi was proof that it is not only the Native American who can harbor an ancient grudge. Crane felt that the Hopi participation in the Pueblo revolt of 1680 and the murder of the Franciscan missionaries was proof of Hopi turpitude. His regime, which lasted for eight years, fueled the distaste among Hopi for Washington and its policies.

In due course, however, more and more was heard in the nation from those artists, anthropologists, and other whites so distrusted by Crane and his fellow agents. Sentiment began to grow in America for Indian people in general. This reached something of a climax at just about the time when President Warren G. Harding's Secretary of the Interior, Albert Fall—who was in favor of a program that would ultimately eliminate the culture of the Indian—found himself rather embarrassed by the Teapot Dome scandal. Fall's financial shenanigans helped discredit all his policies. Eventually, Congressional champions of the Indian began to shape a new policy, which finally led, in 1934, to the Indian Reorganization Act. This essentially codified the obligations of the U.S. government to preserve and protect the rights and heritage of Native Americans. At the same time, with what still seems a heavy hand, it imposed on the tribes a parliamentary form of government, which is now the Hopi organization that deals on a day-to-day basis with the U.S. government as well as the many concerns that living in twentieth-century America requires of even the most remote and private of peoples.

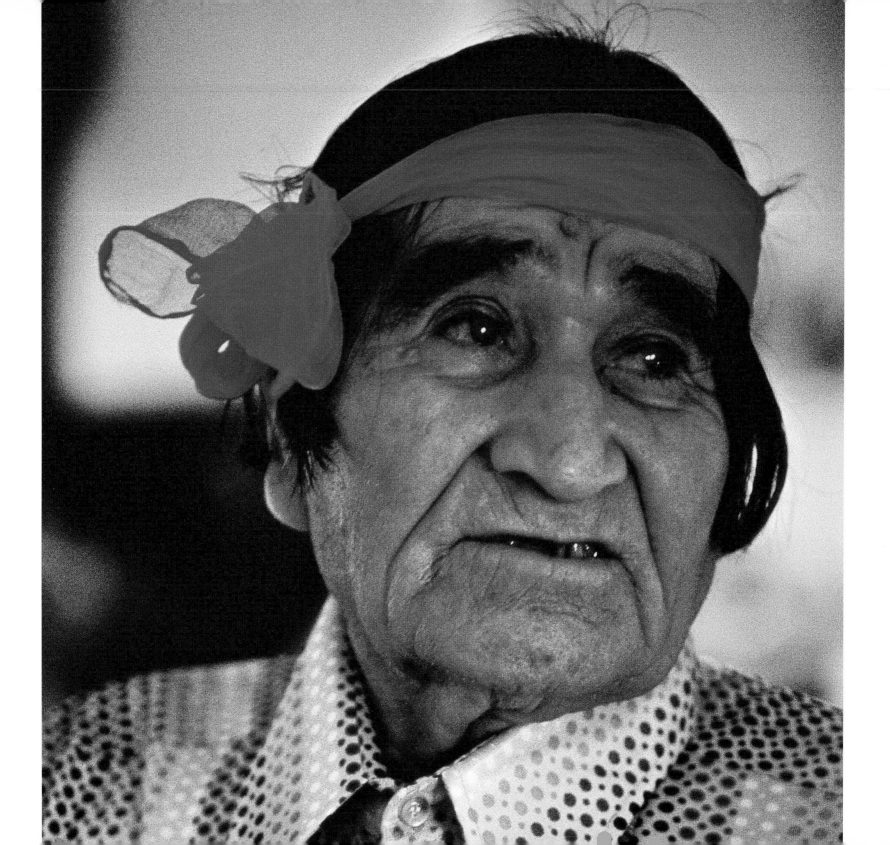

All around, then, there are forces of good and evil,
all vying with one another, all capable of harm
or help to the individual.

AMONG THE SPIRITS

BANG! We woke up in the dark in our room in the Hopi Cultural Center motel. It was one-thirty.

Thump! Tockety, tock, tock.

It was on the roof. Who, we wondered, was throwing rocks on the roof? There were people at Hopi who did not appreciate having us running around taking photographs. We had encountered no particular trouble, though as we were going to bed we had heard what sounded like a snowball hit our window. Maybe, too, the noises were a frozen pipe. It became quiet

Early in the year, Hopi men in certain clans and religious societies go to their traditional eagle-gathering grounds and pray to mother eagles that they will provide offspring to aid Hopi life. If these men have lived well, the mother eagles will indeed be productive. In late spring, carefully selected nephews and other helpers go out to find the eaglets and bring them across the desert to the villages. Hopi consider a young eagle that has never had to hunt for itself innocent and therefore pure—a suitable judge, therefore, of Hopi life. A young hawk has much the same power as a young eagle.

and we went back to sleep.

Bang! We woke up again. *Tock, tockety, tock.*

"What do you think?" I asked.

"Sounds like rocks on the roof, pebbles too," Susanne said.

"Want me to go out and look?"

"No."

Whew.

Bang! It was to be a long night—the first hours of the morning of January 23, 1980. We had spent the previous evening and night snug and warm in a Hopi friend's well-appointed trailer, hung with kachina dolls and etchings of kachinas, and numbering among its conveniences two telephones and an electric typewriter. This was the home and office of Eugene Sekaquaptewa, older brother of the then Tribal Chairman; he was organizing the Hopi Research and Development Corporation, devoted to private economic development on the reservation, at the time.

MESSENGERS • A society in touch with the spirits of the past and the spirits of nature is not inclined to leave matters to chance. Prayer is a familiar form of intercession for the Hopi as it is for many other peoples. At Hopi, prayers are often on the lips of almost everyone—farmers, women preparing corn, children, leaders, and craftsmen. Augmenting a Hopi's personal supplications, the kachinas serve as messengers to the gods, blessing the Hopi with their presence in the plazas during part of the year. But there are other messengers who can intercede. The snakes, which return to the desert after the Snake Dance in August, are messengers. So, too, are the eagles. The eyesight of eagles is legendary, of course, and in most Hopi villages—from early June to late July—eagles and their cousins the hawks sit on the roofs of the houses, observing assiduously the manner in which the Hopi carry out their duties. Like the snakes, they will transmit to the rain spirits their powerful recommendations. One does not, at Hopi, treat an eagle irreverently, for the messages it will later deliver are loud, clear, and precise.

Outside, it was overcast and freezing, snow coming on. The conversation had at one point turned to witchcraft, times when people become suddenly ill. I told a story told to me by an anthropologist who plied another, darker continent and had found himself witched, weakened, sick, and excluded. I explained his theory that witchcraft does work—in the sense of isolating an individual from a close-knit, interdependent society in which everyone relies heavily on being an accepted part of the culture. Witchcraft was, he asserted, an altogether plausible force of psychosomatic potential. Knowing he was isolated from his

A prayer feather and sacred cornmeal on a shrine.

peers, a person might will himself ill, however unconsciously. Eugene nodded and smiled politely, and outside it snowed and snowed. Then a wind came up that rattled the roof of the aluminum trailer, and thunder clapped. At the time it seemed unusual to hear thunder in a snowstorm, but the thought passed as the conversation went on to other matters. Soon we discovered that our low-slung rent-a-car was unequal to the several inches of snow that had fallen in a mere two hours, so we wound up sleeping in the back room of the trailer, with the electric typewriter and a telephone. The next day the road had been cleared and we went about our business.

Then the next night, in our motel room, we continually awakened to the irregular shelling by whatever enemy had taken our roof as the night's target, dozing off fitfully to enjoy a gauntlet of colorful dreams, always knowing half-consciously that we would soon be drummed awake again. Eventually, light began to show through the window, and as the sun made its first appearance over the distant horizon there was a great *BOOM!* and the bombardment was over. I got up grumpily, dressed, and climbed up on the roof to count the rocks, only to find nothing there but thinly crusted snow, crystalline and perfect, undisturbed. Maybe I was crazy, I thought, but both of us…?

Susanne reconnoitered on the ground. Two women in a nearby room had heard the same thing and had been too terrified to sleep at all. Farther along, two men who had been hired to put roofs on some new housing in Kykotsmovi, and whom we had seen around the motel for a couple of days, had also heard it.

"Did you hear that too, man? I mean rocks on the roof—*blam! blam!* I did-

n't sleep all night. What the hell was going on out there, some kind of Halloween?"

Asked if it could have been the roof itself reacting to the cold, he said: "One thing I know is roofs, man, and, they don't make that kind of noise."

Later that day, Alonzo Quavehema listened with great concern to the events of the night. It was not witchcraft, he said after some thought. "If it had been witchcraft directed at you, no one else would have heard it. It's something else."

Another friend suggested that it was a result of the motel's having been built on an old ruin and a trail to a shrine. A Hopi medicine woman told us that, in addition, a line of force or energy—what white people call a ley line—runs along one side of the motel and that these things often happen in such places. They might have been mischievous spirits, adolescents maybe, who had died and did not, for one reason or another, make it to the Underworld. Every now and then they get out of hand. Our friend gave us some piki bread and instructed us to put it on the windowsill the next night; if the spirits came again, we were to tell them to eat the piki and stop fooling around. They did not belong there; this was the wrong place. We went to bed a bit warily that night and fell asleep.

Blam!

Not again, for God's sake! It was eleven-thirty, a half hour before my birthday. *Bang!* I knew it wasn't rocks. The sound was more like that of a hydraulic pile driver: a buildup, like an inhale, and then a massive blast. I knew it wasn't the pipes, because no one builds a plumbing system with pipes running through a roof made of one sheet of plywood and tar paper.

I turned on the light and with theatrical uncertainty ordered whatever it was to go away, to eat the piki bread and leave. I was tired, I explained, and it was, after all, my birthday. I asked Susanne a bit sheepishly if that had sounded about right. She shrugged.

Blam!

At dawn, after opening birthday presents in the weak light of the bedside lamp, the shade of which jiggled with each fusillade of the artillery outside, we were shaken by the last explosion—*Whooobang!*—and the sun rose.

The snow on the roof was still undisturbed. The Hopi woman who was serving as manager of the motel decided to move out of the manager's apartment; her husband had gone to look around the courtyard, hearing nothing, while she had endured the racket inside her room. She would live in the village until her employer, Ferrell Secakuku, did something about it. Ferrell assured us that no harm to us was intended, that the phenomenon was supernatural, just supernatural. It had been known to occur there every now and then, he explained. It was harmless.

After the third night, during which the noise abated slightly, was slightly less violent, it went away. Apparently in response to the urgings of some of the motel personnel, Ferrell had asked a medicine woman from Second Mesa to come and clear the spirits out. She had spent what would have been the fourth night in the motel with her husband but had heard nothing.

Eugene Sekaquaptewa suggested that perhaps it was, after all, directed chiefly at me. Perhaps things go bump in the night, he suggested, to cause a pahana who wants to explain a few things about Hopi to wonder if there are parts of the real world that pahanas have forgotten how to see. You should tell people about spirits, he said, but only what you hear or see. The books by white people about these things at Hopi are mostly wrong.

●

The Hopi land, the Hopi world, is completely peopled with spirits as real as—in fact, part of—the rocks. The sun rises from its house to the east and sets in its house to the west. Then from west to east it travels at night, making it day in the Underworld. The two worlds alternate but are not really separate: they are a continuum. There is a constant reciprocity between them. Spirits of those who have passed on can move readily between the two worlds. The kachinas are "fed" cornmeal and given prayer feathers as "raiment" and enjoined to bring rain in return. Food has its spiritual essence, which can be eaten by spirits. Rain is the liquid spirit—or essence or soul—of clouds, which are in turn kachina spirits in another form.

When people die, they return to the Underworld through Sipapuni and with the aid of Masauwu, the god of death. But certain things must be done properly in their behalf, and there are what might be regarded as side trips to be made before—and even after—reaching the Underworld.

A family we knew had a son named Tony, in his twenties, living away from the reservation in a large city. When we visited the family one day we found them distraught. They had received word that their son had been involved in an accident and had died violently. That had happened on a Thursday night and it was essential to have the body sent back home so that it could be buried by the fourth day, that is, by Monday. But, for reasons that were never made clear, the

police, requiring an investigation before the body could be released, delayed, and the body was returned on Tuesday. Already grief-stricken, the family was nearly hysterical about the timing, since if their son was buried too late he might never be able to reach the Underworld. Immediately upon the arrival of Tony's body, on the fifth day, the appropriate rites took place. His hair was ritually washed with yucca soap, and food was put in his mouth by his aunts. Special food was placed near the grave for the spirits. All Tony's possessions were placed in the grave with him, his aunts added heaps of blankets to keep him warm on his journey, and the grave was sealed.

The family returned to their house, exhausted and anxious. It was an overcast day but nowhere on the horizon was there evidence of rain. No gray streaks of rain united the sky with the earth. People stood around in a kind of daze. Outside, a younger brother nervously dug a shallow pit in the backyard and built a fire in it to roast some corn. A sister tearfully left the house in her car, on her way to her home off the reservation in yet another city.

It grew slightly darker. The wind blew. It began to rain. It rained on the family's house but on none of the neighboring houses—a little circle of rainfall, the drops spattering in the dust and making little cuplike depressions. The family dashed out of the house, literally jumping up and down, laughing with joy.

"It's Tony!" they yelled. "It's Tony! He made it!' They hugged one another and stood in the rain until, after a few minutes, it stopped and left the sky overcast—gray and calm.

As the family had hoped, Tony's spirit had become a cloud and had paused over the family's house and rained on them, to let them know that despite the delay things had been done correctly, the family's hearts had been right, and he was successfully off on his journey. Hopi believe that death is a birth into a new world, the world of spirits, of kachinas, of communication with the living in many ways, and that the living can, if they wish, communicate with those who have passed on. It also rained that night on the cornfield Tony had planted that spring on a visit to the mesas, a field his father had tended through the summer on his behalf. It also rained on Tony's sister as she drove west out of the reservation. But it apparently rained nowhere else. Hopi believe that what seem wayward clouds are often the spirits of departed ones, returning to communicate with the living by raining on their fields; thus they are also kachinas.

Indeed there seems to be a happy mobility enjoyed by the spirits of the deceased—or at least by those who have successfully been "reborn": while they inhabit the Underworld they can also move back and forth with ease, returning occasionally as clouds to bring benefits to their survivors or simply to commune with them. They also inhabit the old ruins where the Hopi clans lived on their way to the mesas, and pilgrimages to such places are expressly for the purpose of communicating with those spirits, to seek guidance and reassurance.

But it is not just the spirits of the successfully reborn who populate the Hopi mesas. There were the troublemakers we had encountered at the Hopi Cultural Center motel; there might also have been Tony. Had his burial not been ritually correct he would have been unable to reach the Underworld, and he would have become lost in time or eternity and doomed to wander around, unfulfilled, in this world, incomplete and unable to be a cloud. It is said that such lost souls can be manipulated by living people who have certain powers—that is, by witches.

A friend of ours told us of a case of witchcraft involving herself. She suddenly found that she couldn't eat—simply could not will herself to put food into her mouth. When she had lost nearly twenty pounds she went to a healer in a nearby village, who divined that she had been witched. He named the witch—a man living at Hopi who apparently thought our friend had been badmouthing him and had retaliated. Through various rituals (not explained to us) and by having the woman eat powdered bear root, the healer removed the force of the witch. Our friend heard later that the witch's wife had suffered the same affliction. Another Hopi woman told us that she had been witched, probably by a sister-in-law who didn't like her, and developed sores on her arms. She went to a healer and the sores disappeared.

Witchcraft seems to be fairly common, but it is not much discussed with outsiders. How one becomes a witch, and for what reasons, we did not find out. Nor did we find out what the punishment is for a Hopi witch who is discovered. Apparently the process of becoming a witch involves very grim duties, including the sacrifice of a relative. Hopi people who steal ceremonial objects and sell them—a terrible violation of Hopi religion and law—are often considered to be witches flaunting their power. Witches enjoy, among other powers, the ability to have out-of-body experiences; disembodied, they can move instantaneously to faraway places. They are rumored to gather, in disembodied form, for occasional conclaves on top of Round Rock, north of Black Mesa, the place where, a dozen years ago, Susanne had been told that Navajo witches meet.

Hopi witchcraft is considered especially strong—as compared, say, to

Navajo witchcraft—and, similarly, Hopi medicine is considered especially effective in fighting off witchcraft. Navajo flock to Hopi medicine men and women. One sometimes hears that those with the power to undo witchcraft also have the power to practice witchcraft.

All around, then, there are forces of good and evil, all vying with one another, all capable of harm or help to the individual. Nor are the spirits restricted to the environs of Hopi.

In January 1982, we accompanied the new Tribal Chairman, Ivan Sidney, and several other Hopi to Washington, to the Smithsonian Institution's National Museum of Natural History, where the curator of North American ethnography had graciously agreed to show us some of the Hopi artifacts (collected around the turn of the century) in its care. He led us up the stairs to the fourth floor at the top of the great rotunda, where a door opened into a long dusty corridor, lit by naked light bulbs here and there. Along one wall was rack after rack of Zuni pots; on the other side, row upon row of cabinets. Eventually we reached the cabinets with "Hopi" labels, as well as little tags that said "Poisoned," in reference to the fact that the artifacts had been sprayed to keep insects away.

As drawers were opened, one of the Hopi, a priest, sorted through the objects, while the others stood off at a slight distance. The Tribal Chairman explained that the priest had carried out a special ceremony beforehand to keep evil forces away, so that he could touch the objects. Later he would purify himself. Susanne noticed a distinct odor and asked if it was bear root. The Tribal Chairman said yes, they were all chewing it.

The priest examined several drawers of artifacts, pointing out that some were

not Hopi but Zuni in origin. The curator took notes. In one drawer they found a collection of odd-looking bundles with tassels of what looked like straw coming out of one end. The Tribal Chairman explained that they were witchcraft devices, used in very grim rites, and that they should have been buried long ago, after they had been used. No good, he said, could come of having them here.

In another cabinet they found several objects associated with kachinas, wrapped in clear plastic bags. The priest said the bags should be taken off, since the kachinas could not "breathe" with them on. When the bags were removed, the Tribal Chairman said that with so much pent-up energy released, the city would experience a mammoth snowstorm within four days.

A day later they decided to cut their visit to Washington short by two days because of their feeling that something bad might happen. With a raging snowstorm virtually stopping all the traffic in the city, they took the Washington Metro to the airport, passing under 12th Street by the National Museum of Natural History. Half an hour later, at just that spot, another Metro train derailed and three people were killed in the accident. The Hopi arrived at the airport to find that a jetliner had failed in its takeoff, crashed into the 14th Street bridge, and plunged into the ice-bound Potomac River, killing more than seventy people. The Hopi felt the energies released in the Smithsonian must have played a role in these tragedies.

More than ever, they feel that such artifacts as those they had just seen should be returned "home" from museums and private collections around the world so that their spirits, possessors of such long memories, could find rest.

Everything, then, has its own spirit. That is why Alonzo Quavehema was so

To capture a young "cottonhead" golden eagle, a youth, attached to a cable, is dropped over the side of 300-foot-deep Canyon Diablo. He swings himself into the eagle nest and attaches a rope to the eaglet, which is hauled up to the rim, where it is greeted by relatives of the man in charge of the hunting party. Sometimes the eaglet is placed in a cradleboard for its trip to the village, where it will become a member of the family.

LEFT: Hyeouma coming up out of the nest.

clan to gather eagles, but in this particular case Valjean took other relatives along to help. Typically, in order to catch the young eagle a boy is lowered by hand over the side of the cliff on a rope, but this time Valjean had borrowed a four-wheel-drive truck with a winch. The men fashioned a rope harness for one of the boys, hooked it to the steel cable, and lowered the boy over the side until he could step onto the ledge with the eaglet on it. The boy tied a rope to the flapping bird's legs and sent it aloft. The boy was then reeled in, and the eaglet was placed in a box in the back of the truck, shielded from the sun's glare with a shirt. The eagle gatherers patrolled the rest of the canyon but found nothing and returned home, arriving after dark.

Before dawn, the morning after the eagle's arrival, Valjean's female relatives entered the room and, one after another, took in hand a perfect ear of white corn—the eagle's Mother Corn—selected from Valjean's stores of corn, and washed its head and back with a mixture of clay and water. It was given a name from Valjean's clan—Hyeouma ("Spider coming down")—and from that moment on it was a member of Valjean's family.

Hyeouma was placed in a second-story room for a few days and was soon moved to the roof, where it sat, tethered to a wooden perch. There were four other eagles on the roofs of Shungopavi that summer. Some years there are more, other years fewer. By the time of the Home Dance, in late July, Hyeouma had lost his fluffy white "cottonhead" and was nearly full-grown—a sleek, dark-brown eagle with fierce eyes that watched the comings and goings of the people of Shungopavi and periodically called out in high-pitched tones. Hyeouma was a noisy bird.

The eagles are supposed to live on the roofs of the houses where their new families live, since they are literally members of the families. We heard of a man who kept his eagle on a building where no one had lived; the following year he was not given an eaglet by the mother eagles. When a baby eagle is taken from the nest, a gift is left behind for the mother—a piece of turquoise or a polished seashell. It is not unusual, we were told, for the mother to come and visit the eaglet on the roof. A friend told us of an eagle that was kept untethered on a roof in Mishongnovi. It would fly around during the day, often following its owner as he drove to work in his pickup, and return at night to be fed. Hyeouma got loose one day that summer and flew off over the village to the mesa's edge. And instead of taking off over the desert, it flew right into the arms of the boy who had collected it from the nest and just happened to be standing there. The boy covered Hyeouma with a shirt and brought the eagle back to Valjean.

Bird lovers (among whom we number ourselves) and conservationists often wince when they hear of the Hopi's use of eagles. Are they not endangered species? We discussed this with Edward S. Ayensu, director of the Smithsonian Institution's Biological Conservation Office. "The eagles are an important part of their religion," Dr. Ayensu said, "and the Hopi have been using eagles this way for hundreds of years in the same area. You would have to say that the Hopi are among the best eagle managers we have, in the sense of wildlife management. It is not the Hopi who have put eagles on the list of endangered species. It is our civilization, with its highways, mines, deforestation, pesticides, and hamburger stands." And now, it appears, it is also the Navajo.

RIGHT: A season's eagles keep their vigil atop the houses of Shungopavi.

FOLLOWING PAGES: Hyeouma at Home Dance with the kachina's gifts. An eagle gathered by Burt Puhuyestewa being named in the manner of a human baby.

On the first day of the Home Dance in late July, two months after Hyeouma's arrival in the village, the kachinas gave the eagle a small coiled plaque, a bow and arrow, a small kachina doll, and some piki. These were placed at the eagle's feet, just as toys are given to the Hopi children by the kachinas. Since one cannot be sure of the eagle's sex, it is given the traditional toys of both girls and boys.

Susanne was to photograph Hyeouma on the morning of the second day of Home Dance, but Valjean was extremely nervous about it. He was the kiva chief for the dance; he was ultimately responsible for seeing that there were good feelings on the part of everyone in the village. Susanne's presence on the roof, even at dawn, before most people were up and about, and before the kachinas emerged from the kiva, might cause controversy, which would contaminate the entire ceremony. Valjean decided against this last photograph. Valjean's father-in-law, Viets, a man in his late eighties and one of the most respected elders in the village, lived with Valjean and his wife. It was too important, Viets said, for the world to see the whole story of the eagle—of this eagle. It should be photographed. Valjean acceded, aware that he risked a great deal. At dawn, he took Susanne on the roof for about twenty seconds.

That evening, after the ceremony, we were sitting on the front porch of Valjean's house. Viets was sitting hunched up in a chair, chatting with some neighbors. Presently Valjean walked out on the porch; the kachinas had gone home to San Francisco Peaks. Viets looked up at his son-in-law and said, "There's the only brave man."

Soon thereafter, Valjean and his helpers "sent Hyeouma home," smothering the eagle in cornmeal, and took it to its burial place. They removed all its feathers except those on the head and two primaries, one on each wing. They buried it with its gifts from the kachinas, with prayers that its spirit should soar away and confirm to the other spirits that the Hopi had done well, that their ceremonies had been carried out properly, and that it could rain on their fields.

But Hyeouma's spirit would remain in the village, too, and also find its way to many of the sacred shrines of the Hopi. Hyeouma's wing and tail feathers would be fashioned into ceremonial objects and used in the village for generations. The down feathers would become pahos, prayer feathers that would bestow blessings on shrines and on many people in the village and elsewhere.

On the day we left Hopi that summer, Valjean made two pahos from Hyeouma's down feathers and those of a flicker and gave them to Susanne, instructing her that one should be hung in our living room and one in our car to keep us healthy, safe, and prosperous.

A couple of small piles of rocks located
on the rubble-strewn top of the Peaks are as important to the
Hopi as, say, St. Peter's is to Roman Catholics.

·········· THE **LAND** ··········

IT IS CALLED *tusqua*, "the land." It extends from Tokonavi (Navajo Mountain, across the border in Utah) to the point on the New Mexico border where Route 40 leaves Arizona, to the northern edge of the White Mountain Apache Reservation, to Bill Williams Mountain, west of Flagstaff, to the rim of the Grand Canyon, where the long trail begins that winds down to the Havasupai Indian Reservation. By far its dominant feature is San Francisco Peaks, eighty miles southwest of the Hopi mesas, the ancient volcanic home of the kachinas and thus the site of the Hopi's most important shrines. This large area is the ancestral land of the Hopi.

San Francisco Peaks and much of surrounding Coconino County are in the charge of the National Forest Service, and since 1962 a modern ski lift

·········

Prayer feathers and a pouch of sacred cornmeal lie atop a rock near a shrine. Carvings on the surface record the date of a recent pilgrimage to the site and various clan emblems; the concentric circles are an ancient migration symbol.

has brought many recreationists to the Peaks' west side. The lift and the lodge are operated by a local business, Northland Recreation, of Flagstaff. In late 1980, Northland Recreation sought to exercise its right to build five more ski lifts on the Peaks, and in May 1981 the Hopi tribe and the Navajo Medicine Men's Association (who also regard the Peaks as sacred) joined with Richard Wilson, a non-Indian owner of adjacent land, to file suit against the Forest Service to stop further development. The suit was brought under the American Indian Religious Freedom Act and would be heard by Judge Charles R. Richey of the U.S. District Court in Washington, D.C.

One of the points raised by the Forest Service in a pretrial hearing was that Hopi priests on their way up the Peaks to their shrines had used the ski lift to shorten their trek, thus legitimatizing it. So on the day in the summer of 1981 when Susanne accompanied Dalton Taylor and Fred Kootswatewa, a young man who worked in the Tribal Chairman's office, to the shrines on

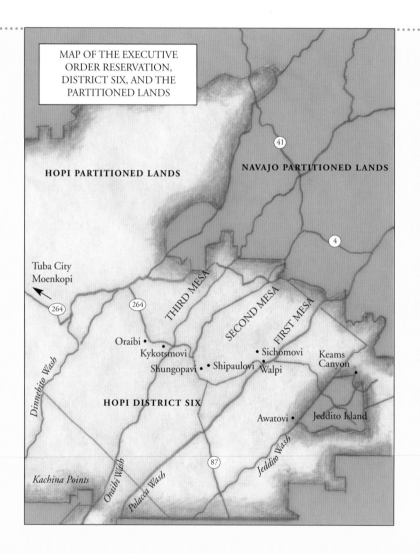

MAP OF THE EXECUTIVE
ORDER RESERVATION,
DISTRICT SIX, AND THE
PARTITIONED LANDS

HOPI PARTITIONED LANDS

NAVAJO PARTITIONED LANDS

41

4

Tuba City
Moenkopi

264

264

THIRD MESA

SECOND MESA

FIRST MESA

Oraibi •
Kykotsmovi •

• Sichomovi

Keams
Canyon

Shungopavi • • Shipaulovi • Walpi

•

Dinnebito Wash

HOPI DISTRICT SIX

Awatovi • Jeddito Island

Kachina Points

87

Oraibi Wash

Palacca Wash

Jeddito Wash

top of the Peaks, they hiked the entire way: from the ski lodge, which is at about 9,000 feet, past the top of the ski lift, at about 11,500 feet, to the top, 12,363 feet. They stopped at the first shrine, hidden in a pile of lava boulders, and Dalton kneeled and prayed, placing a paho in the small hole, sprinkling it with cornmeal, and smoking his pipe over it.

They had planned to go only to this first shrine, but since they were so near, Loren decided that they should press on to the second one, at the top of the highest of the peaks ranged around the old crater. Several hours later, at the second shrine, Dalton repeated the ritual, and they paused to look out over the landscape that spread away from them. There was a haze, partly the result of forest fires some 600 miles to the west, in California, and the Hopi mesas were invisible. Before leaving the top, Dalton filled his canteen from a patch of snow that still clung to the scree. On the way down, Susanne asked if she could have a drink of the icy water, and Dalton gave her the canteen. As she drank, Fred, with a certain look of nervousness, offered Dalton a drink from *his* canteen. Susanne stopped in her tracks with an awful realization. The snow in the canteen was not for drinking but for some sacred purpose. She apologized, and Dalton waved it off. "It's all right," he said, and they continued down the mountain, returning to the lodge ten hours after they had started out. "Typical," Susanne said afterward. "Dalton was simply too polite to refuse."

Afterward I talked about the problem of San Francisco Peaks with Eugene Sekaquaptewa, brother of the then tribal chairman. "What you have to understand," he said, "is that the kachinas have a great deal to do when they are at home up there. They have to rehearse; they have to practice bringing rain. You

THE SACRED BOUNDARY

Cartography is not a Hopi art. Rather, Hopi read the features of the land, knowing the look of a butte from several directions in several kinds of light, the degree of erosion of a cliff, or how the passage of several generations of wild animals through a place makes a slight depression in the sandstone. And so, when the Hopi go forth periodically to visit the ancient shrines that mark the spiritual boundaries of that part of the continent where they know they belong, they do not need a map. They address the spirits of the place, pledge their everlasting concern, and listen to the messages that provide them with the strength to endure.

Every so often, a group of Hopi men set forth to travel the perimeter of their ancestral land and make prayers and offerings. Sometimes, also, they go individually to clan shrines located in the ancient hinterlands, places that previous Hopi have marked in stone, crossroads of the clans as they gathered long ago. And often, to collect herbs, evergreens, and messages, they go to the top of San Francisco Peaks, near Flagstaff, one of the homes of the kachinas and a source of Hopi life and its survival.

can see from here that there are usually clouds over the Peaks. Well, I suppose scientists—you know, meteorologists—would explain it their way, but the Hopi believe that what is going on is the kachinas, the spirits, rehearsing. And if a lot of people start walking around up there, it will interfere. The kachinas are very—what would you say?—very polite, and they would be trying to keep out of the people's way, instead of rehearsing."

Later that summer, Judge Richey decided in favor of the Forest Service on the main issue of the protection of Indian religious freedom. (On a matter

Practically everywhere one goes in the Hopi lands and their surroundings, one finds old (and new) clan symbols and, rising up from the earth, ancient potsherds.

relating to the National Historic Preservation Act, he ruled in favor of the tribes and remanded the case to the Forest Service.) The Hopi and the Navajo Medicine Men's Association sought an appeal, and at the same time filed a motion to present newly discovered evidence. It must, of course, be difficult for someone living in Washington, D.C., where the most prominent feature of the landscape is the cluster of high-rise office buildings a mile away, in Arlington across the Potomac River, to imagine how near the Hopi are to the Peaks even though eighty miles separate the Peaks from the Hopi mesas. It is probably impossible for most people to realize that a couple of small piles of rocks located on the rubble-strewn top of the Peaks are as important to the Hopi as, say, St. Peter's is to Roman Catholics. Progress has its own dialectic, though, and development of the Peaks seems inevitable: the ski lodge will probably get its liquor license, more lifts will snake up the side of the mountain, a fast-food joint will adorn the upper reaches of the Hopi's modest cathedral, and a swarm of condominiums will be constructed at the gate to the sanctuary.

The loss of ancestral lands is nothing new to the Hopi, or, for that matter, to most other tribes in North America. The Hopi sustained their first—and greatest—loss in 1882 when President Arthur, by executive order, assigned them a rectangle of some 2,400,000 acres in approximately the middle of the large area the Hopi refer to as "tusqua," the land. At that time, there were approximately 2,000 Hopi within their newly specified borders. Since that time, and until recently, the history of the additional loss of Hopi land is strictly a matter of Navajo encroachment, which has been essentially disregarded by the U.S. government.

To understand what has happened in the intervening years, it is necessary to go back in history. Before 1840 the chief problem the Hopi faced from outside was raiding by other tribes. Ute bands would cross the San Juan River and sweep in to raid Hopi cornfields, then withdraw to their territory in the north. Apache would do the same, from their area in what is now central and eastern Arizona. It is highly unlikely that any Navajo laid eyes on San Francisco Peaks before about 1700; the first Navajo raids on Hopi were in the 1840s.

The Navajo are Athabascan stock, related to the Athabascan Indians of Alaska and Canada. So are the Apache. Indeed, it is only in the last few centuries that the two languages—Navajo and Apache—became mutually incomprehensible. When the Spanish arrived in New Mexico, the Navajo were simply a discrete population among many Apache groups, inhabiting an area northwest

of the Rio Grande pueblos. All these people had come down from the north, probably subsequently to the permanent settling of the Hopi mesas. In any event, the people who came to be called Navajo arrived as nomadic bands of hunter-gatherers and, being extremely adaptable, began to elaborate a highly sophisticated worldview and culture, borrowing freely from the Pueblo people, upon whom, in the manner of nomads, they also preyed. They must have moved into the area of the Rio Grande before the middle of the sixteenth century, for there is evidence of their raiding before the arrival of the Spaniards and the horse…and the sheep.

Twelve years after the Pueblo rebellion of 1680, the Spanish returned to New Mexico. The people of the Rio Grande pueblos and the Spanish worked hand-in-glove to solve what had become the number one problem of the area— the Navajo. The "Pueblo auxiliaries" outnumbered the Spanish soldiers by about five to one—volunteers, not conscriptees, seeking to free their lives of the omnipresent threat of raids by the Navajo.

Having adopted the horse, the Navajo had become far more efficient raiders. The introduction of sheep gave them an economy. And observing the Spanish social structure, they evolved from small, loose-knit bands into a class society, wherein individual Navajo leaders became wealthy to an unprecedented degree, owning millions of sheep, which were tended by other Navajo in return for the use of the sheep as needed. Under this oddly feudal system the population was able to grow, and the Navajo extended the territory they inhabited throughout western New Mexico. (Meanwhile the Apache and Comanche, both of whom persisted in being merely raiders, never achieved the kind of economic base that would enable them to support larger and larger populations. Their raids continued, but their numbers remained much the same.)

By the time—in the 1830s—that revolution had expelled the Spanish from Mexico and had put New Mexico into the hands of the Mexicans, the Navajo were without question the main destructive force in the Rio Grande area. The Spanish and the Pueblo auxiliaries had simply not been up to the task of containing them. The Mexican government in New Mexico was almost totally feckless, and for a couple of decades the Navajo, universally feared terrorists, were rampant throughout the area.

In the 1840s Mexico lost New Mexico to the United States. Among the first tasks of the territorial government of the United States was to bring peace to the area, which meant among other things to stem the incessant depredations of the Navajo. In due course, Kit Carson, the famed mountain man, was dispatched to round up and subdue the Navajo, a task that he discharged with ruthless efficiency. A great number of Navajo—about 8,000, representing approximately two-thirds of their entire population—were rounded up and marched 400 miles across the territory of New Mexico to Bosque Redondo and kept in what is sometimes called a military encampment but was in fact an early version of the concentration camp. This was the infamous Long Walk. Several years later a treaty was concluded and the Navajo were marched off, westward across New Mexico, and settled on a rectangular piece of land of approximately 3,000,000 acres lying athwart the Arizona-New Mexico border. The Navajo promised in their treaty to remain on that reservation.

LEFT: A youth high up on the cliffs in Canyon Diablo in quest of an eagle.

RIGHT: Over the millennia, artists have left symbols and pictures on the rocks—records of their presence with meanings lost.

In a letter to me on this subject, Abbott Sekaquaptewa reviewed some of this history:

"Only a few Navajo had settled in Hopi country before Kit Carson's campaign. According to U.S. government reports (which were made as a result of repeated appeals for aid by the Hopi and constant friction between the two tribes), there were only 300 Navajo—men, women, and children—in the area set aside by President Chester A. Arthur on December 16, 1882. An earlier survey reported that the *westernmost* penetration of the Navajo in 1848 (in terms of settlements) was a north-south line that is located approximately at the present-day junction of the Chinle road with Arizona State Route 264, a few miles west of Ganado. This agrees with Hopi tradition about the territorial boundaries of the two tribes. This is also the same location where a Hopi, Ta-uo-pu (Pobe) by name, was killed by Navajo out on a plundering mission. Subsequently, this event involving the killing was used to designate the territorial boundary. After 1848 and after Kit Carson started his campaign, the Navajo began going beyond the line into Hopi territory, because *they were in flight to escape Carson. They were hiding out from Carson, not settled there.*"

It seems that the Navajo's feudal system was crushed by the demeaning years at Bosque Redondo in eastern New Mexico and by the sequestering in the reservation land which their leaders acceded to when they signed a treaty with the U.S. government. But they began to move west as their population grew. As Sekaquaptewa wrote, "It was after 1868, *after the treaty,* that they began settling in Hopi territory, outside their treaty reservation, and in violation of their treaty with the U.S. *and* a separate treaty with the Hopi."

Around this period the Hopi and the Navajo did formally agree to certain boundaries for the two tribes—those referred to by Sekaquaptewa—and part of the formality of the treaty signing was the conveyance to certain Hopi chiefs of a ceremonial object called the *tiponi.* (About one hundred years later, when the two tribes once again met to discuss the matter of territory, the village chiefs of First Mesa, who had been entrusted with the tiponi, produced it as a proof of the old agreement. Apparently, the Navajo denied its importance, though one of them offered to buy it.)

The Navajo continued to move into the Hopi Reservation, and the Hopi continued to complain to the U.S. government, to no avail. Raiding and thievery continued, as the government agents' reports testify, but chiefly the problem was that Hopi were effectively denied the use of much of their land. Each year it became more restricted, though Hopi cattle-owners occasionally ranged as far south as Leupp and east to Ganado.

In the 1940s the Bureau of Indian Affairs (BIA) intervened and decided to treat the Hopi and Navajo reservations as one administrative unit, dividing the entire area into nineteen Land Management Districts, or Grazing Districts, at the same time instituting a massive across-the-board stock-reduction program. Many Hopi refused to move their cattle and were promptly arrested. With the Hopi cattlemen out of the lands to the west of the mesas, the Navajo moved in, disregarding the new grazing regulations. Most of the 100-odd Navajo who had encroached on District Six (one of the nineteen Land Management Districts, comprising 600,000 acres) were moved out; the refusal of some to leave led to a lengthy court battle that saw them evicted after ten years.

One can perhaps sympathize with the BIA of those days and its confusion about how to make Native American cultures fit into the limited number of pigeonholes in a rolltop desk, and one can understand its effort to reduce over-grazing and the destruction of the land. Both tribes found the stock-reduction program outrageous, and the Hopi continued to complain to Washington, to no avail. Ultimately, in 1962, a three-judge federal court ratified the arrange-ment, ruling that District Six was exclusively for the Hopi and that the remain-der of President Arthur's rectangle was to be considered a Joint Use Area (JUA) for the two tribes, to be "shared and shared alike." This case, *Healing* v. *Jones*, was termed "the largest quiet title case ever tried." Thus was a deeply important cultural decision made on the basis of principles of animal husbandry.

"Joint use" effectively meant sole Navajo use of the lands outside District Six. Indeed, it meant incursions of Navajo livestock into the Hopi's exclusive area, and in the early seventies the Hopi began impounding Navajo sheep that strayed over their boundary, as was, of course, mandated by law. This tended to heat up the dispute.

Joint use also meant that both tribes would share in the mineral rights to the land within the Executive Order Rectangle. But in the mid-sixties, in the words of Abbott Sekaquaptewa, "the Navajo Tribe, unilaterally and without telling the Hopi Tribe, granted a coal exploration permit to the Sentry Royalty Company (predecessor of the Peabody Coal Company) to conduct a strip-mining opera-tion at the north end of Black Mesa. We, the Hopi Tribe, found out and through legal challenges forced the Navajo Tribe and the BIA to make us a party to the permit issuance and a subsequent lease agreement. They agreed to it only because we would have gone to court and stopped the whole thing." Whether Peabody's Black Mesa coal mine will ultimately prove a long-run benefit for the Hopi remains a moot question. It sharply divided the Hopi at the time, with the traditionalists joining forces with regional environmental groups to wage a bat-tle against Peabody, which they eventually lost.

In any case, the event—as it is thus described by one of the participants—makes it clear that there was little likelihood of useful negotiation between the two tribes over the far more complex and ancient problem of the land. To remedy the continuing disregard of Hopi rights in the Joint Use Area, the Hopi sought relief: more orders were issued, which the Navajo rejected, incurring a contempt citation and a $250,000 fine. Steadfast in their disregard for the law, Navajo leaders refused to acknowledge the rights of the Hopi in the Joint Use Area.

In partial recognition of this, and also of the fact that the United States had erred over the years in letting the Navajo overrun the Hopi Reservation, Con-gress passed a bill in 1974 providing that the Joint Use Area should be cut in half—one half for the Hopi and one for the Navajo. That law (known as the Navajo-Hopi Settlement Act) was the result of numerous hearings, hundreds of exhibits, months of lobbying by Navajo and Hopi, thoughtful compromising by committee staffs, and studies by senators and congressmen. The two tribes were to negotiate the new boundary, and if such negotiations failed, a federal judge was to draw the line. Negotiations under the supervision of a carefully selected federal mediator stretched out over nearly nine months but failed, and the line was drawn, a tortuous line that is itself a graphic symbol of the long and bitter conflict. Neither side was totally satisfied with the final boundary. The

Shipaulovi, nestled at the very highest point of Second Mesa.

Navajo would lose 900,000 acres, and about 750 families would have to move. The Hopi regained 900,000 acres for their own exclusive use, leaving them 900,000 shy of what President Arthur had designated for them. One Hopi told me how they thought about it: "Suppose someone all of a sudden decides to camp in your backyard, and stays there. You try and get him to leave but he won't. Finally you get a judge to deal with the matter, and the judge says that since he was in your back yard for so long he can have half of it to live on."

On one of our early visits to Hopi, we were taken by plane around the area. The twin-engine jet hurtled above the desert at about 200 miles an hour. I looked out the window and felt uneasy. I turned to Nathan Begay, who was in charge of land management in the BIA office in Keams Canyon. Nathan is a Hopi, but his father was a Navajo. I asked him what our altitude was. He looked out calmly and said: "Let's see, we're about eight feet over the trees. I'd say fifteen feet altogether."

We were flying an early morning mission of the Hopi Border Patrol, hugging the contours of the land and following a newly built fence, an early portion of the fence that would one day reproduce on the ground the line the judge had drawn to partition the Joint Use Area. It was 1977, and things were a lot calmer than they had been earlier. Nathan told me that one Navajo had tried to shoot the border patrol plane out of the sky on one of its earlier runs.

"You see how green it is on our side of the fence," said Nathan, "and how brown it is over there? That's sheep. Every now and then a Navajo will bring his sheep over to our side, where the grazing is better. You should see them scatter when we fly over them at this altitude."

The airborne border patrols were discontinued shortly afterward because Navajo trespass into District Six had all but ceased. Once the Hopi ordinances were enforced, and the Navajo knew they would be enforced, the Navajo controlled their animals and stopped the trespass. There have been demonstrations—about 800 Navajo marched into Keams Canyon in the summer of 1981, led by Tribal Council Chairman Peter MacDonald, who made a speech and laid a wreath against the BIA offices. (The BIA superintendent, Alph Secakuku, kept the wreath, "but I don't know what it's supposed to mean," he said.) There have been threats of violence and there have been some violent events—mostly pushing matches between Navajo women and the people building the fence; on a few occasions construction workers have been shot at.

The 1974 partition order called for a number of things. First, there was to be a stock reduction campaign to rid the seriously overgrazed Joint Use Area of the overburden of sheep. A fence was to be built. And several thousand Navajo were to be relocated (about 100 Hopi were also to move). It is the relocation of people—it began with about 6,000 and has risen, as of the beginning of 1982, to over 9,000—that has become an emotion-laden factor in the Navajo resistance to the congressionally ordered solution. It remains a highly political issue in the state of Arizona.

In the summer of 1980 the Navajo were paid a visit by a Phoenix apartment-building entrepreneur named Bill Schulz, who spent an afternoon with some of the people who had to relocate. He reported that he was "mightily moved," and was thereby given an extra injection of energy in his effort to unhorse Senator Barry Goldwater, one of the prime movers of the 1974 legislation. If elected, he would write a new bill undoing the damage to the Navajo. The Navajo Tribal Council promptly met and endorsed Schulz by a vote of 72 to 0. This was no empty endorsement, since the numerous Navajo (there are now about 150,000) have often provided the margin for a candidate to win or lose in Arizona. During the meeting, a councilman named Freddy Howard rose to speak, "Many Navajo subject to relocation have vowed they will not move despite federal marshals, despite the U.S. Cavalry. What they will do is hard to predict." He went on to compare the "forced" relocation to the Long Walk.

One can forgive Howard a bit of exaggeration, perhaps; after all, the Navajo district that he represented was now on the Hopi side of the line. And the Long Walk was unquestionably a brutal piece of business. Kit Carson may be lionized in the Southwest by whites, but he was a pretty difficult fellow, and one cannot help thinking that he took delight in being nasty to the Navajo. On the other hand, the federal government is offering a new house (worth about $70,000) and a considerable cash payment (some $5,000) to each Hopi and Navajo family caught up in this unsatisfactory affair so that they can, by 1986, comply with the requirements of the law. An administrative body has been set up—the Hopi-Navajo Relocation Committee—to oversee all this, and while bureaucracies are generally unresponsive; they do not ride horses behind the oppressed, hitting old Navajo women up the sides of their heads if they don't hustle along to prison.

Nevertheless the complaint of the Navajo tribal government is heartrending, for relocation is a painful process. Tribal Council Chairman MacDonald has vowed to take the matter to the public, to resist all efforts at stock reduction or at relocation in the hope that Congress will undo the damage. The Navajo tribal government has budgeted half a million dollars a year for the public relations campaign that has been launched.

The administration of this entire matter has been allowed to grind to a halt—essentially in order to let tempers cool. The livestock-reduction program has been replaced, on the order of the Secretary of the Interior, by a livestock grazing-permit program, allowing ten sheep (or the equivalent) per Navajo adult on the controversial land. Twenty sheep per family is more, one BIA official told me, than the officially determined carrying capacity of the land.

The argument will probably go on for some time, and it seems therefore worthwhile to review the details. The Navajo say that the U.S. government, by building schools and other installations for the Navajo on the former Joint Use Area, has de facto recognized the Navajo right to live there; in effect, it has "seen fit to settle" them there. Why should Navajo be asked to leave now? The people living there, they say, have a deep religious attachment to the land and are the most traditional Indians in the country.

The Hopi may have been in the region first, but, to quote Chairman Mac-Donald, "The Navajo belonged to the land—long before the land belonged to either the Navajo or Hopi under Anglo law." He argues that the Hopi have never made use of the land in question, but now a small minority of them want to take the land back in order to swell their cattle herds. Thus it is an issue of cattle over people. It is a question, also, of legal rights over human rights. It is improper, further, for the U.S. government to punish Navajo for mistakes the government itself confesses it made. When it was seeking to resolve the issue in 1974, Congress was uninformed about the economic and human costs of relocation. Tribal Council

Vice-Chairman Frank E. Paul says, "To force 9,525 people to become refugees in 20th century America is an act of cultural genocide which will be a blot on the conscience of the United States Government."

The Navajo have complained that this Hopi "land grab" is to benefit Hopi cattle owners at the expense of Navajo people. There are a few mom-and-pop cattle ranches at Hopi—about 100 head each—but not many Hopi families run cattle, and that is because there has been little room for them to do so within the confines of District Six. To say that people are being replaced by cattle, however, is not accurate. Sheep will be replaced by cattle in a very few instances, and people by other people.

Currently in the Joint Use Area there are eight times as many Navajo animals, mostly sheep, as the land can support. In 1972 there were about 120,000 sheep in the Joint Use Area, and by 1979 there was no visible reduction, this despite the government's reduction program, whereby one could sell off livestock at 150 percent of the market value. In those seven years the government bought 150,000 head from the Navajo. In 1981 the President's Council on Environmental Quality pointed out that the Navajo Reservation is one of the three worst examples of desertification in the United States.

Plans are afoot for a new Hopi village to be built on Howell Mesa, northwest of First Mesa, providing room for the slowly growing Hopi population—which is now about 10,000—and perhaps providing jobs for people who would otherwise have to live off the reservation, partly for lack of space in District Six. And of course, the Hopi do use the land, as we have seen, for a variety of purposes, most of them bound up with their ceremonial needs.

BELOW: The desert's bounty requires special seeds, backbreaking labor, and constant spiritual engineering.

RIGHT: Yucca stalks dry in the sun, later to be dyed and become plaques.

Near Tuba City, along the ancient trail that Hopi leaders have taken for hundreds of years to the Grand Canyon to collect salt for ceremonial use, there are some boulders with clan symbols, long strings of figures carved into the stone, marking all the times the Hopi have passed by. One of these rocks now has graffiti scratched over it.

The chief benefit to the Hopi of reacquiring some of their land will be that some of their shrines will be returned to their care. A small fraction at least of the tusqua, where for a millennium the Hopi clan leaders have gathered herbs and ceremonial objects essential to the core of their life, will be under their sole jurisdiction and may escape defacement and destruction.

That relocation is an awful strain is not in question. How great a strain it is remains moot. One of the strongest statements on the subject, often adduced by the Navajo government in support of its claims, was made by Professor Thayer Scudder of the California Institute of Technology, who in March 1979 released a report under the auspices of the Institute for Development Anthropology, Inc., of Binghamton, N.Y., a private research group.

Professor Scudder, two graduate students, and six research aides interviewed 118 Navajo during the Christmas break of 1978 to ascertain the amount of stress that relocation, or the threat of relocation, was placing upon them and to assess their ability to cope with it. He found the stress severe and their ability to cope with it overtaxed. Marriages were breaking up; people were getting drunk; there was a whole range of psychological ill effects occurring among these people. Scudder recommended that the 1974 act be repealed and the Navajo be allowed to buy the Joint Use Area land. He said that Congress had been sadly uninformed as to the

true nature of the strain of relocation, that human rights were seriously violated, that old people in particular (everyone over forty, in fact) were under severe stress, since their grandchildren would have no place to go, and that Navajo elsewhere on the reservation were also placed under a severe strain by having their lands crowded by relocatees. In the summer of 1980, Professor Scudder summarized the devastating conclusions of his study in a letter to President Jimmy Carter.

There are a few problems with all this, some of them being what social scientists call methodological. For example, five of the researchers engaged in the interviewing process were Navajo. Of these, four were employed at the time by the official Navajo land dispute committee. Scudder admitted that no effort was made to get a random sample; instead, the interviewers just spoke to whomever they came across during the Christmas recess. Further, social scientists have pointed out that, in this situation, 118 subjects are too small a sample from which to make statistically valid extrapolations and generalizations.

There is also a problem about the scholarly responsibility for this report. When queried, the president of the Institute for Development Anthropology, Inc., said the institute was not involved and had not participated in the study, and that the opinions arrived at were not those of the institute.

There are questions of content as well. Navajo, like all Indians, have marital problems, drinking problems, and other psychological problems. In fact, so do non-Indians. Relocation cannot be considered the sole or even a major culprit. In several instances the data in the Scudder report simply do not support its conclusions. Of twenty-nine Navajos who had moved to off-reservation urban sites, twenty-four had positive things to say about relocation. The vast majority

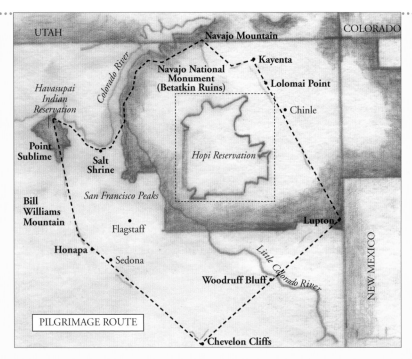

UTAH · COLORADO

Navajo Mountain

Colorado River

Kayenta

Navajo National
Monument
(Betatkin Ruins)

Lolomai Point

Havasupai
Indian
Reservation

Chinle

Point
Sublime

Hopi Reservation

Salt
Shrine

San Francisco Peaks

Bill
Williams
Mountain

Flagstaff

Lupton

NEW MEXICO

Honapa

Sedona

Little Colorado River

Woodruff Bluff

PILGRIMAGE ROUTE

Chevelon Cliffs

of relocatees interviewed "did not think that it was worse in any way for their children since relocation."

As for the stress due to taking Navajo back onto their own reservation, by the end of 1979 only about 5 percent of the few hundred people who had been relocated had joined their relatives on Navajo land—hardly what would be perceived as a welcoming attitude of a people for its own kin.

Finally, on the question of Congress not being properly informed of the stressful effects suffered by the Navajo, it should be noted that Dr. Scudder

himself testified before both a federal court and the Senate Interior Committee as all this was brewing and said on those occasions exactly what he said in his 1979 report. A renowned expert on relocation in Africa, at the time of his testimony he admitted to not being an expert on the Navajo.

It is time now for a little cultural mathematics. If there were 300 Navajo on the Executive Order Reservation in 1882, and the growth rate for the Navajo population is 2 percent a year (Scudder's estimate, accepted by the Navajo) then how many Navajo should be there now? About 2,220. And how many are there? More than 12,000. This means that in the past hundred years more than 10,000 Navajo relocated there from somewhere.

There are, the Navajo say, 14,000,000 acres of Navajo land. That is about the area of Connecticut, Massachusetts, Rhode Island, and New Hampshire combined. Two percent of that is 280,000 acres. This means that to satisfy the requirements of, the Navajo population and culture, that is, to enable the Navajo to pass on to their grandchildren that which they are entitled to under ancient Navajo tradition, they would have to be assigned each year vast amounts of land—280,000 acres, an area one-third the size of Rhode Island—the first year alone.

Those who invoke history should be prepared to abide by its inescapable lessons. The Long Walk, now regularly invoked by the Navajo, was without doubt another sorry entry in the white man's long record of inhumanity to the continent's prior inhabitants. People so wronged should never be wronged again. In the case of the Navajo, however, this appeal simply does not wash. Kit Carson may have been a sadist, but the foremost duty of the U.S. government was

unquestionably to keep the peace between all the Indians and the whites. It was not the Pueblo people of the Rio Grande, or the Zuni to the west, or the Hopi even farther west, whom Kit Carson was told to subdue and control. It was the Navajo. This is by no means to suggest that the Navajo culture is unchanged from those old marauding days, or that they should have to pay now for their cultural style at the time.

But it is interesting to note that while the Hopi tusqua was shrunk first to 2,400,000 acres and then to 600,000 acres, the Navajo now have 14,000,000 acres, so that they are probably unique among Indian tribes in the United States in having far more land now than when the white man arrived. It is also interesting to note that the Hopi population has grown from 2,000 to 10,000 in the centuries since the whites arrived, while the Navajo population has grown from about 12,000 to 150,000. The Hopi economy and culture are in relative balance with nature. Hopi land, though under stress, remains remarkably productive; on the other side of the fence is a near moonscape of dust and weeds. The Navajo culture, for all its wondrous qualities and for all its fine people, remains rapacious and out of balance with the biological resources available to it.

It may be that the Navajo tribal government has not served its people well in this matter. For example, in an area north of District Six called Big Mountain a group of Navajo developed a deep, unshakable resistance to relocation. The Hopi Tribal Council offered to swap: the 20,000-odd acres constituting the Big Mountain area could be given back to the Navajo in return for sixteen small parcels elsewhere along the partition line. The sixteen parcels were all vacant—except for two dwellings on one parcel—and their combined acreage would be equivalent to the Big Mountain area. The Navajo government refused on the grounds that the Big Mountain area was used for grazing sheep—an odd stance for people who deplore animals being considered more important than people.

It is not at all clear what the ultimate outcome will be. The Navajo will continue to resist; a new U.S. government administration preoccupied with budgetary matters might choose to welsh on the federal payments to relocatees. Or the government may indeed proceed to carry out the intention of Congress and some of the original Hopi land may be returned to them.

The situation is complicated in some minds by another kind of settlement—that made with the Hopi by the Indian Claims Commission. The commission was established in 1946 to hear claims for financial recompense for lands taken away from the various tribes. At the time there was no Hopi Tribal Council—it had been disbanded in 1940, after operating fitfully for about four years—and the Hopi brought no claim before the commission. However, in 1950 a group of Hopi elders journeyed to Washington to see if a claim could be pressed and were told that their only hope was to revive the Tribal Council. This was done, with seven villages sending representatives to its meetings, just in time to engage a lawyer and submit an official claim before the deadline.

Matters ground on slowly, and in the 1970s the Hopi were awarded $5 million for land they had lost. This caused considerable controversy among Hopi, the traditionalists claiming that the Tribal Council had sold out the Hopi's right to their ancestral land for a mere $5 million—about five to six hundred dollars per Hopi. This is not actually the fact. The $5 million was for the land's value computed as of the time it was lost, and most of the land was lost when

President Arthur established the Executive Order Reservation. But more to the point, the Hopi have given up only the right to return to the federal government and ask for more money for lost territory; and in fact they had negotiated an offer of $3 million up to $5 million. Even more important is the fact that the Tribal Council and the U.S. government agreed to disagree as to just what the boundaries of the land in question are. Nearly one million acres of the previously confiscated territory for which the Hopi were paid were restored to the Hopi under the partition of the Joint Use Area, and other litigation is in process through which the Hopi seek to regain additional lands surrounding the 1882 area, including the land around Moenkopi and Tuba City, which has been in dispute since 1934.

That the Hopi will ever regain ownership of the original Hopi tusqua is obviously out of the question, nor is this really what they seem to have in mind. In 1951, leaders of nine religious societies in Shungopavi—traditionally the village most concerned with the land—presented a statement to the Commissioner of Indian Affairs outlining the boundaries of their traditional lands. In part it said:

THE HOPI TUSQUA IS OUR LOVE AND WILL ALWAYS BE...

1. It is from the land that each true Hopi gathers the rocks, the plants, the different woods, roots, and his life, and each in the authority of his rightful obligation bring to our ceremonies proof of our ties to this land. Our footprints mark well the trails to these sacred places where each year we go in performance of our duties.

2. It is upon this land that we have hunted and were assured of our rights to game such as deer, elk, antelope, buffalo, rabbit, turkey. It is here that we captured the eagle, the hawk, and such birds whose feathers belong to our ceremonies.

3. It is upon this land that we made trails to our salt supply.

4. It is over this land that many people have come seeking places for settlement, and finding Shungopavi established, asked our leader for permission to settle in this area. All the clan groups named their contributions to our welfare and upon acceptance by our leader were given designated lands for their livelihood and for their eagle hunting, according to the directions from which they came.

5. It is from this land that we obtained the timbers and stone for our homes and kivas.

6. It is here on this land that we are bringing up our younger generation and through preserving the ceremonies are teaching them proper human behavior and strength of character to make them true citizens among all people.

7. It is upon this land that we wish to live in peace and harmony with our friends and with our neighbors.

We realize that within the area of the Hopi land claim there are towns and villages of other people. It is not our intention to bring disturbance to the people of these places, for our way requires us to conduct our lives in friendship and peace, without anger, without greed, without wickedness of any kind among ourselves or in our association with any people; and in turn to have guaranteed that there will be no disturbance to us in the carrying out of our traditional life....

BELOW RIGHT: Priest Dalton Taylor smokes a clay pipe in prayer at one of the shrines at the top of the San Francisco Peaks, where the kachinas rehearse the bringing of rain six months out of every year.

Each year, Hopi make many pilgrimages throughout the ancestral land: to eagle shrines, clan shrines, ruins, special markings, salt sources, to San Francisco Peaks, and to myriad other places, many of them secret, to pray for the continuance of Hopi life. Perhaps the most important pilgrimage is one made not every year but periodically, when selected priests travel to the shrines that denote the boundaries of the Hopi ancestral land. Such a pilgrimage had been scheduled for September 1980. When we had accompanied Valjean Joshvema and Alfred Joshongva on their eagle hunt, Alfred, who was the leader of the Wuwutsim society, had concluded that it might be a good idea for us to accompany the priests and document their activities. Alfred himself would not be able to go, since at the time of the pilgrimage he would have just gone back to work in a road crew, but Valjean agreed that we should go along. And so it was arranged—or we thought it was.

A few days before the pilgrimage was to begin, we were told by Fred Kootswatewa, whom (with Dalton Taylor) Susanne had accompanied to the top of San Francisco Peaks, that there would be a meeting that night in Shungopavi to make the final arrangements, and that we were to attend. Accompanied by Fred, we drove to Dalton's house. There, gathered around the kitchen table in the dim light, were some people we had met—Valjean, Nathan Begay from the BIA office, and Percy Lomaquahu from Hotevilla—and some we had not. We were introduced and sat down on a couch across the room. The men talked in Hopi. Presently the door opened and George Nasafti, the old Bluebird Clan leader, limped in. He had led the pilgrimages in years past, but his health would not permit him to go on this one. There was a great deal of conversation, some of

Dalton Taylor, aided by Fred Kootswatewa, inspects a second shrine on the Peaks, one of the most important Hopi sacred places. The kachinas have to compete for space here with tourists and skiers.

it apparently heated, some of it containing the telltale word pahana, and then George turned to us and said: "What is it that you want to photograph?"

"Whatever you want us to document for you," Susanne answered, explaining that we would use some of the resulting pictures in a magazine article and a book, but only those that the Hopi wished us to use; after this the photographs would be given to the Hopi for their permanent archives. There was more conversation in Hopi, and then, in English, various logistical arrangements were made. After the meeting, we stepped outside into the darkness, and Fred said: "That was close." We asked him what he meant. It seems that a number of the men there, including Dalton, who was to lead the pilgrimage, had been unaware that we had been asked to join the pilgrimage. Our coming along had to be justified while we sat there, and Susanne's answer to Goerge Nasafti had been what had tipped the scales in our favor. There would be six priests, plus Nathan Begay and Fred as drivers. This meant that at the end of the pilgrimage there would be only twelve living Hopi (including other priests not scheduled to go on this particular pilgrimage) who had seen all the shrines marking the ancestral land—and two white people.

Before dawn on the appointed day we assembled at Dalton's house; there were three vehicles, two trucks and a van (driven by Alph Secakuku, the BIA superintendent and one of the six priests). The caravan started down the road out of Shungopavi and stopped before reaching the highway. Dalton stepped out of the lead vehicle and sprinkled cornmeal from a small leather pouch along the side of the road and placed a paho in a nearby bush. Then we were off on a trip that would take four days and cover 1,100 miles.

The first leg of the trip took us south and east for two hours to Lupton, a small town near the New Mexico border. We had driven through the dawn in relative silence, broken only by an irritating cough I had developed. North of the highway at Lupton, huge red cliffs loomed up, and we parked near one of them and made our way back into the mouth of a great canyon, past wavy lines and other symbols carved into the face of the red sandstone walls—clan markings from the time of the gathering of the clans. A dry wash snaked along beside us. We stopped and Dalton began digging in the sandy earth next to the rock face. This place, we were told, is called Nah-mee-toka by the Hopi. Soon Dalton found some sticks, the remains of pahos from previous pilgrimages. He put these into a wooden box that Nathan Begay had brought along, and then new pahos were placed in the box and it was set in the ground. Dalton, followed by the others, took cornmeal from the pouch and sprinkled it over the pahos, praying in Hopi. They asked if we would like to say a prayer and gave us some cornmeal to sprinkle in the shrine. Afterward, the men sat around the shrine and smoked their clay pipes, passing them back and forth, each time saying the word that signified the relationship of the person receiving or giving the pipe—uncle, father, son. Each man kneeled and blew smoke into the box. The ceremony at an end, Dalton put a wooden lid on the box and covered it with dirt.

Formerly, Nathan explained to us, the pahos had been placed on the ground, but they had sometimes been disturbed or taken. So the practice had begun, a few years back, of burying them. The wooden boxes were an innovation introduced this year, to preserve the pahos longer.

BELOW: On a pilgrimage made periodically over the last thousand years to shrines that mark the extent of the Hopi ancestral land, selected priests leave a shrine near Lupton, on the New Mexico border, at which, generations ago, Hopi clans left their marks.

RIGHT: North of the Hopi Reservation, in Navajo National Monument, is a restored village ruin called Betatkin—in Hopi, Ky westima. Located deep in a canyon, it was an ancestral home during the gathering of the clans. The shrine itself (*near right*), overgrown by grass and brush, was found near the face of the cliff below the ruin.

Back in the truck, Percy Lomaquahu turned around in his seat and handed me three small twigs. "Chew them, one at a time, until the taste goes away," he instructed. I did, and within minutes my cough had vanished. They were from the roots of a young cedar tree he had seen along the way.

We drove north hour after hour, skirting the eastern edge of Black Mesa, past Lolomai Point, on to Navajo National Monument (Ky westima), some thirty miles south of the Utah border. The National Park Service attendant was expecting us, Nathan Begay having notified him the day before, and said that if we waited until four o'clock—about fifteen minutes—the last tourists would come out of the canyon and he would close the monument for us while we went down. The little exhibit at the top of the canyon explained that the ruin down below was called Betatakin and had been inhabited by people ancestral to the Hopi. At four we began the trek down into the canyon, a 1,500-foot descent along a winding trail of rocks and manmade steps placed there for the benefit of tourists. Along the way, Alph Secakuku pointed out a large round face carved into the rock about a hundred feet above us. "That's Masauwu," he said.

On the canyon floor we walked about a mile along a trail that cut through a lush forest of evergreen trees and cottonwoods until, coming around a corner, we saw a huge vaulted cave, formed by an enormous overhang in the red rock wall. Located high in the cave was an old ruin, with red stone houses, perhaps thirty altogether, perched precariously upon one another, with long rickety ladders connecting the various levels. On a ledge below the ruin we paused while the shrine was located; then the ceremony took place as it had near Lupton, while the ghosts of the ancient village no doubt looked on. As we left I won-

dered how some of the older priests—in their sixties—would make it back up the 1,500 nearly vertical feet out of the canyon. Indeed, I wondered how Susanne and I would make it.

Ky westima was a place where Virgil's people had lived on their way to the Hopi mesas. It was also the place where some of his people were supposed to return after the split at Oraibi in 1906. That night, after we had driven another few hours and had made camp, up near the Utah border, and had eaten roasted corn and fried chicken around a huge fire, the other men teased Percy at length about his people's inability to reach Ky westima. All the other priests were from Second Mesa, and we were told that this is because Shungopavi had the chief responsibility for the ancestral land, Oraibi having at one time or another become too sympathetic to the pahana.

We woke before dawn, and the sky was deeply overcast. Without breakfast we broke camp and headed for Navajo Mountain—Tokonavi—across the border in Utah. It began to rain, and the mountain was shrouded in dark, fast-moving clouds. Water trickled down the narrow dirt track that led up the mountain, and the men went on foot ahead of the four-wheel-drive truck, throwing rocks into deep ruts and taking boulders out of the road, but finally to no avail: the road proved impassable. In a dark glen beside the road, Dalton founded a new shrine to serve until another pilgrimage reached the one on top in some other year, and while the ceremony was taking place, Nathan Begay chipped a series of concentric circles into a boulder to mark the location. On the way down the mountain, torrents of water cascaded over the rimrock and the road was awash for miles. It was a disappointment, not reaching the top, but the rain was a good sign.

The next stop was several hours away, a ledge a few hundred feet down in Grand Canyon, below Grand Canyon Village; this was not one of the territorial shrines but a place the priests traditionally stopped at to pray for the sacred salt that is located in a deposit on the canyon floor near the confluence of the Colorado River and the Little Colorado, the location also, the priests told us, of Sipapuni. This was the only reference—and they made it so casually—to the place of emergence into this world, perhaps because it all seems so obvious and natural to them. From there, we went to Po ta ve taka (Point Sublime), a drive of several hours west through a state park and then through seemingly endless meadowland, to the narrow and rocky beginnings of a canyon that leads down circuitously to the reservation of the Havasupai Indians, the beginning of the Havasupai Trail. At the end of the track, the point at which no vehicle invented by man could have gone farther, there was an ancient automobile, its windows and most of its floor gone, a comical skeleton of a dominant society—a failed attempt, it seemed to me, to reach the wrong goal. The priests went off on foot, down into the canyon, arriving eventually at a great overhang in the gray cliff wall. As Dalton sought the shrine, the others looked at an excavation, an illegal one—the carefully dug rectangular hole that is the sign of the pothunter. Nearby, on a rock upon which the priests placed their pipes and cornmeal pouches, were what seemed to be fresh rock carvings of clan symbols. "That is

where," they said, "we made our marks last time." There was an eagle boldly carved in the boulder.

"Is that yours?" I asked Percy.

"No, that is Abbott's," he answered. "He came with us last time." Abbott walks on two aluminum crutches, making his way painfully even along flat surfaces. I couldn't conceive how he had made it down to this place which we had reached only by scrabbling on hands and feet, like goats. Though Tribal Chairman, he had no particular clan office that would have made it necessary for him to see these shrines. He had nothing but the determination, I thought, to be certain that he had seen with his own eyes those things that were crucial to Hopi survival, so that he could say to congressman and senators and anyone else who saw fit to intervene, "I've been there."

The priests conducted the ceremony of placing feathers in the shrine, and also cornmeal, and then smoking, as the sun went down. We left, driving into the dark to the state park, where under a roof-covered stove made of stone beside a group of picnic tables we cooked a late meal and went to sleep to the sound of the rain.

The following day, we woke up in the rain. Most of the priests had slept in the trucks; Susanne and I had stretched out on the picnic tables. In the dark, I saw Alph Secakuku, shirtless, pouring water over his head.

"How'd you sleep?" he asked.

"Like a baby," I said. "How about you?"

"Well, *I* managed to get through the night without wetting my pants!" he replied. There were guffaws from the gloom. The fire was started, and we

Midway through the four-day pilgrimage, the priests made their way into the Grand Canyon
to the place where a trail starts to wind its way down to the Havasupai Indian Reservation, one
of three reservations that abut Grand Canyon National Park. At the shrine the men smoke
ceremonial tobacco in clay pipes.

roasted corn and chiles and set off for Bill Williams Mountain, a peak that lies west and north of Flagstaff. In the charge of the Forest Service, this is another eagerly eyed location for ski lifts. During the previous pilgrimage, when the priests had carried out the ceremony, they had run into an old man, a bearded fellow who seemed rather like the old mountain man of the 1830s for whom the mountain had been named; he had said he would watch over their shrine and make sure no one disturbed it. He was a Forest Service employee, apparently responsible for whatever duties are performed by such lonely people in such a lonely, out-of-the-way places. The Hopi had been pleased. This shrine is called Tusak Choma.

When we reached the pine-scented peak of Bill Williams there was no old man, but the shrine was intact and Dalton found seven old prayer sticks. The prayers said, we descended the mountain and headed for Honapa (Bear Springs), located near a marsh an hour away, down a little-traveled series of dirt roads west of Sedona. It took a considerable amount of time to find the shrine, for this one had only recently been identified, through the memories of George Nasafti and the reconnoitering of Nathan Begay. There had been a period—some ten years or so—when the Hopi had not made these pilgrimages, and it had taken a great deal of searching by Nathan and George to locate this most obscure shrine. It was now carefully marked and easier to find; upon our arrival, the ceremony took place and the priests climbed back in the trucks and drove south a long way.

Eventually, late in the day, we reached a place known as Chevelon Cliffs or, by the Hopi, as Sak wai vai yu: it is also known as Apache Trail. "We should call this Hopi Trail," said one of the priests. Walking through a stand of massive

pines, scattered here and there among meadows of wildflowers, we came on a gray igneous rock that had a spiral chipped into it. Beyond the rock, Dalton dug and found the pahos of the earlier pilgrimages, and the ceremony again was performed. That night, as we camped nearby, what little conversation took place in English turned on the prevalence of bears in this area. Susanne slept on top of the truck; I slept in the front seat.

The next day, on our way to Woodruff, Arizona, and the last shrine, we stopped off at a nameless rock formation and clambered up a cliff into a three-foot-high slot in the rock, on the ceiling of which were a number of ocher paintings of men and animals. The place had recently been found by one of the pilgrims during a personal expedition into the terrain, and he wanted us to see it.

At Bill Williams Mountain, west of Flagstaff, priests perform their ritual over the shrine, placing prayer feathers in the ground, sprinkling sacred cornmeal over the feathers while praying, and blowing smoke directly into the shrine. The prayer feathers are made of eagle down and flicker feather affixed to a stick. (In recent times the prayer feathers have been placed in a wooden box to keep them safe from vandalism.)

One series of paintings showed a few men standing near another who had been impaled with a spear. The Hopi priests calculated that this spot was on a straight line between Chevelon Cliffs and the last shrine in Woodruff. They wondered if the pictograph did not suggest that this had been a Hopi outpost in ancient times, and that it was here that the Hopi had at one time sought to repel invaders.

Shortly thereafter we arrived at the foot of a nearly symmetrical hill outside Woodruff. We drove partway up, to a point where a metal fence enclosed a collection of electrical transformers, and the priests began the trek to the top. Valjean Joshvema, whose age and poor health had forced him to stay on top of the canyon at Ky westima, stayed below with the trucks, gazing off into the distance beyond a pair of mesas on the horizon to Lupton, where we had first stopped four days before. On the top of the hill the priests found the rocks that had been inscribed with the spiral-shaped migration symbol, and they performed the same ritual over the shrine. In the course of the pipe smoking, Alph Secakuku passed me his pipe, a clay one in the form of a mountain lion. I smoked it and passed it back, saying: "I suppose this means I can't make fun of you anymore."

"No," he said, "it means that you can call me *kwaatsi*. You are not a Hopi, and you have no clan, so when you receive the pipe you can't say 'uncle' or 'son.' But you can say 'kwaatsi.' That's the Hopi word for friend. Kwaatsi. When you say 'Ikwaatsi,' that adds emphasis."

Late in the afternoon, several hours after we had left the bluff above Woodruff, called Tsi mun tu qui, the caravan approached Shungopavi and stopped. Dalton emerged from the lead truck and prayed, then retrieved the paho from the bush alongside the road, and the pilgrimage was over. All that was left was for Dalton to report to the Bear Clan leaders of the village that he and the others had visited the shrines and prayed over them and had encouraged the spirits of those places to be aware that the Hopi had done well.

The priests learned later that after we had left the Grand Canyon area and

Woodruff Bluff is the last stop on the pilgrimage. The shrine on the bluff is endangered because it is on private property, and the owner could allow the top of the bluff to be used in highway pavement.

the Havasupai Trail, it had rained so hard that the Park Service and the local authorities had had to shut the area down to tourists. The priests had done well.

The shrines and the former dwelling places, a Hopi told me, are the physical monuments of their domain—the standards, just as the United States flag is the standard of the government and the nation. They are the permanent boundary markers of the Hopi tusqua, and the knowledge that they remain, brought back from time to time to Bear Clan leaders who cannot ever see them, provides assurance that the Hopi will continue as a cultural entity. They are, for now, watched over by the feathers of an eagle named Hyeouma, his "father" being one of the priests on the pilgrimage and his feathers bearing the Hopi offerings to the spirits of the shrines. They will be guarded by other eagles' spirits in the years to come, in the active hope that the Hopi way of being true citizens among all people will survive. And I would wager that the Hopi will survive us all, as their prophecies foretell, and that lodged precariously on their mesas, where they and they alone belong, they will be reminders, as long as we will listen, that while there are many ways to live on the land, the only true way is to honor it. To look upon it and say: How awesome, how demanding, how generous.

And the rest of us…we would do well to seek a way that requires us to "conduct our lives in friendship and peace, without anger, without greed, without wickedness of any kind, among ourselves or in our association with any people." And in this endeavor perhaps we might all find a way to guarantee that there will be no disturbance to the Hopi in carrying out their traditional life.